ALL-TIME BOX-OFFICE HITS

This book was devised and produced by
Multimedia Publications (UK) Ltd.

Editor: Richard Rosenfeld
Assistant editor: Sydney Francis
Production: Arnon Orbach
Design: Michael Hodson Designs
Picture Research: Vivien Adelman, Sheila Corr

First published in the United States of America 1985 by Gallery
Books, an imprint of W.H. Smith Publishers Inc., 112 Madison
Avenue, New York, NY 10016

ISBN 0 8317 0289 3

Typeset by: Letterspace Ltd.
Origination by: Imago
Printed in Italy by: Sagdos, Milan

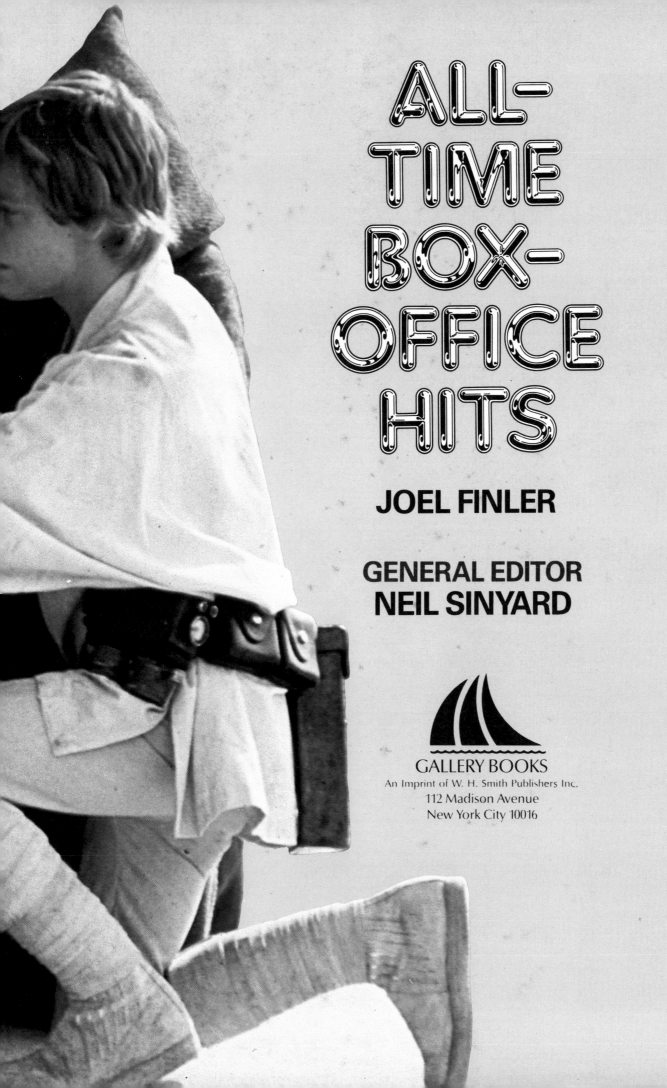

ALL-TIME BOX-OFFICE HITS

JOEL FINLER

GENERAL EDITOR
NEIL SINYARD

GALLERY BOOKS
An Imprint of W. H. Smith Publishers Inc.
112 Madison Avenue
New York City 10016

CONTENTS

Introduction	**6**
The Thirties	**12**
Grand Hotel	22
The Kid from Spain	
Roman Scandals	24
42nd Street	26
She Done Him Wrong	
I'm No Angel	28
San Francisco	30
Modern Times	32
Little Women	34
Snow White and the Seven Dwarfs	36
The Adventures of Robin Hood	38
Gone with the Wind	40
The Forties	**42**
Sergeant York	54
Mrs Miniver	56
Random Harvest	58
Cat People	60
Meet Me in St Louis	62
Going My Way	64
Spellbound	66
The Jolson Story	68
The Best Years of Our Lives	70
Duel in the Sun	72
The Fifties	**74**
The Robe	88
From Here to Eternity	90
Shane	
Giant	92
How to Marry a Millionaire	
The Seven Year Itch	94
The Ten Commandments	
The Greatest Show on Earth	96
Around the World in 80 Days	100
Peyton Place	102
The Bridge on the River Kwai	104
South Pacific	106
Ben-Hur	108

The Sixties	**110**
Psycho	120
The Sound of Music	122
Doctor Zhivago	124
Thunderball	126
The Dirty Dozen	128
Bonnie and Clyde	130
The Graduate	132
2001: A Space Odyssey	134
Butch Cassidy and the Sundance Kid	136
Easy Rider	138
The Seventies	**140**
Love Story	150
The Godfather	152
The Sting	154
The Exorcist	156
The Towering Inferno	158
Jaws	160
One Flew Over the Cuckoo's Nest	162
Star Wars	
Close Encounters of the Third Kind	164
Saturday Night Fever	
Grease	168
Superman: The Movie	172
All-Time Box-Office Hits	174
Conclusion (The Eighties)	**180**

Opposite: *Scarlett O'Hara (Vivien Leigh) in green dress watches Rhett Butler (Clark Gable) dance in* **Gone With the Wind** *(1939).*

Endpapers: *A helicopter attack in Vietnam in* **Apocalypse Now** *(1979).*

Page 1: *The idol in the Temple from* **Indiana Jones and the Temple of Doom** *(1984).*

Pages 2-3: *Luke Skywalker (Mark Hamill, kneeling) and R2-D2 (left) in* **Star Wars** *(1977).*

INTRODUCTION

This book gives an account of the most popular movies ever made. As such, it is both a history of the film industry and a survey of popular taste. Through an introduction to each decade, it outlines box-office trends and also the broad cinematic and social contexts in which these movies were made. This introduction is then followed with a closer look at the most popular movie within a particular genre, in every case trying to account for the popularity of these pictures.

That little something extra
In some cases, even in retrospect, the box-office appeal of certain movies is hard to explain. At times it seems as if audiences are drawn by stars and, at other times, it seems as if stars make very little difference. At times certain genres are extremely successful (like the epic blockbusters of the fifties) and others not so popular (for example, war movies and westerns during the thirties and seventies).

There are undoubtedly reasons for this, which can range from the commercial to the sociological. It is plausible to see movies in a certain period as representing a kind of psychology of a decade. The critic Robin Wood has described popular Hollywood movies as a "dream-like expression of an American collective unconscious". But do movies *create* a demand, or supply one? Ultimately, box-office appeal is as elusive to define as star quality, unless one borrows James Mason's definition of the latter in *A Star Is Born* (1954) as "that little something extra". That "something extra" could be a performance, a title song, the script, the direction, color, topicality, or a combination of all these, or something else entirely. The essays on the individual movies can be seen as a search for that magic ingredient.

A Star Is Born (1954) plots the rise and fall of two contrasting careers. Alcoholic film star (played by James Mason) spots a future star and, as it turns out, wife, when he sees band singer (Judy Garland) performing at a charity gala. Later, he traces her back to a nightclub where he finds her rehearsing the aptly titled song "The Man That Got Away". However, while her career rockets towards the Oscars his deteriorates, culminating in suicide.

The selection of individual movies for discussion has been determined both by popularity and profitability. For example, although *Cleopatra* (1963) took more money than most movies during the sixties, it cost more than any, and almost destroyed 20th Century-Fox: to include it as a box-office hit entirely on the basis of its rentals would have been grotesque. Conversely, although movies like *Cat People* (1942), *Psycho* (1960) and *Easy Rider* (1969) are not amongst the massive money-makers, their huge profits in relation to their modest cost more than justifies their inclusion. The statistically minded reader will notice that each introduction concludes with a list of the Top Ten money-making films of the decade, and the Top Ten box-office stars. The placings of the movies are based on gross domestic rentals in the United States and Canada, as estimated by *Variety*; the box-office star placings are based on data from *Variety* and the *Motion Picture Almanac*.

Left: *Elizabeth Taylor as* **Cleopatra** *(1963). The film cost $44m, but recovered over half of this from domestic rentals, rising to twentieth in the all-time box-office hits.*

Below: ***Easy Rider*** *(1969) with director Dennis Hopper (left) as Billy, and producer Peter Fonda as "Captain America"; a small-scale budget movie that made a handsome profit.*

Right: ***Psycho*** *(1960) was Alfred Hitchcock's biggest hit. Production costs of $800,000 were topped by domestic rentals of $11.7m. He shot it cheaply, in television style.*

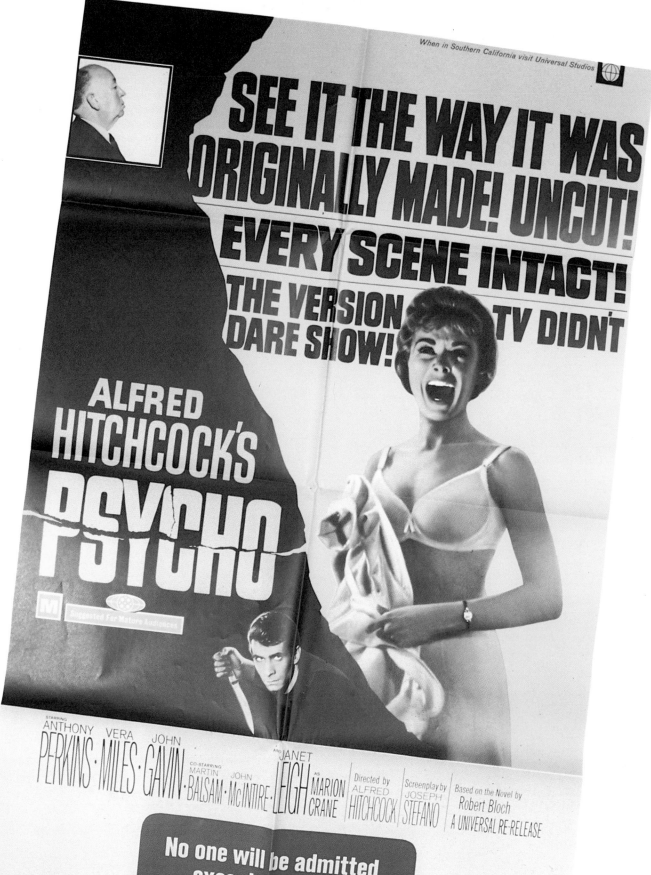

Pull of the stars

Although the survey starts in the thirties (for no movie made before then figures in the Top Fifty list of *Variety*), the basic pattern of the movie industry and its economic organization had been established during the previous decade. Production was in the hands of the major studios. The star system flourished. Then as now, the public flocked to see their favorites – Mary Pickford in *Daddy Long Legs* (1919), Rudolph Valentino in *The Sheik* (1921), Lon Chaney in *The Hunchback of Notre Dame* (1923). It was a great era for comedy, in which the popularity of Chaplin in movies such as *The Kid* (1921) and *The Gold Rush* (1925) was rivalled by the bespectacled acrobatics of Harold Lloyd in *The Freshman* (1925). But how would such slapstick athleticism manage to cope with the talkies?

Oscars were awarded for the first time in 1929, and it was not long before the industry would see the commercial value of such awards. A director like King Vidor, who had had an enormous success with *The Big Parade* (1925), found he could still flourish in the coming era of sound and the studio system, but a more unusual and rebellious directing talent, Erich von Stroheim, found he could not. The most popular movie at the end of the twenties was still D. W. Griffith's saga of the American Civil War and its aftermath, *The Birth of a Nation* (1915), and it was to remain so until David O. Selznick's saga of the Civil War and its aftermath, *Gone with the Wind* (1939). Interestingly, some of the biggest successes of the period, like *The Four Horsemen of the Apocalypse* (1921), *The Ten Commandments* (1923), *Ben-Hur* (1925), *King of Kings* (1927) were all to be remade during Hollywood's crisis period of the mid-fifties and early sixties. But, technologically and commercially, the twenties had crises of its own. Our story begins with the coming of sound, and the Wall Street Crash.

Left: *Charlton Heston took the role of Moses in Cecil B. DeMille's 1956 remake of his own **The Ten Commandments** (1923) when Theodore Roberts had played the silent Moses.*

Two of the cinema's greatest ever box-office draws. **Right:** *Rudolph Valentino as **The Sheik** (1921) – he repeated this portrayal in **Son of the Sheik** (1926), his last film.* **Top far right:** *Charles Chaplin shown on a contemporary poster for **The Kid** (1921). This was his first feature film and featured child star Jackie Coogan.*

CHAPTER ONE:

THE THIRTIES

The thirties began with the Great Depression and ended with the outbreak of the Second World War, and the political and economic uncertainties of the period were clearly reflected in the film industry. Financially, technologically and socially, the thirties was a traumatic time for Hollywood. Financially, nearly all of the studios (with the exception of the star-studded MGM) had a difficult period during the worst years of the Depression up to 1934. The studios were still coming to terms artistically with sound, and were now having to deal with developments in color. Socially, Hollywood was trying both to reflect the life of Depression America and provide escape from it; and endeavoring to capture the cynicism and realism of the period whilst at the same time not run foul of the censor. It was sometimes a difficult balance to maintain, and not surprisingly quite a few producers veered too strongly away from the compromise.

With everyone under contract, from the biggest star to the lowliest technical assistant, each studio tended to develop its own recognizable style. Throughout the thirties, MGM was the glamor studio. "More Stars than there are in Heaven" was their claim, based on their impressive line-up of actors and actresses under contract – Garbo and Gable, Crawford and Harlow, Shearer and Tracy. They were committed to stylish escapism in pictures like *Grand Hotel* (1932), *Mutiny on the Bounty* (1935), *The Great Ziegfeld* (1936) and *San Francisco* (1936), and the glossy MGM look was developed by supervising art director Cedric Gibbons and costume designer Adrian, who, along with other leading designers of the period, provided the stars with fashions which were admired and imitated all over the world.

Top right: *Jewel thief (John Barrymore) falling in love with a suicidal ballerina (Greta Garbo) in Irving Thalberg's magnificent production of **Grand Hotel** (1932).*
Right: ***San Francisco** (1936) was a fine piece of stylish Hollywood escapism in the charming company of Clark Gable as the saloon owner and Jeanette MacDonald playing the ambitious singer.*
Opposite page: *In **The Great Ziegfeld** (1936), "A Pretty Girl (Virginia Bruce, top) Is Like a Melody", at least according to Dennis Morgan who mimed to Allan Jones' well-trained voice.*

A life of crime is not much fun for Paul Muni (above) *about to be freed by his chain-breaking pal in* **I Am a Fugitive from a Chain Gang** *(1932), or for Edward G. Robinson* (right), *as gangster Rico in* **Little Caesar** *(1931).*

The gangster as hero

Warners had a different outlook. When Darryl F. Zanuck became production head in 1930, he said his production policy would be planned around headline news. Out of this policy emerged a topical classic like *I Am a Fugitive from a Chain Gang* (1932), starring Paul Muni, which reflected the despair and despondency of a nation. More famously, a string of contemporary gangster films like *Little Caesar* (1931) and *The Public Enemy* (1931) not only made stars out of Edward G. Robinson and James Cagney, respectively, but seemed, controversially, to make stars out of the gangsters they played as well. The gangster hero was a romanticized, individualist rebel who struck out at society, providing a Depression audience with a kind of vicarious revenge against a social system that seemed to have betrayed their hopes.

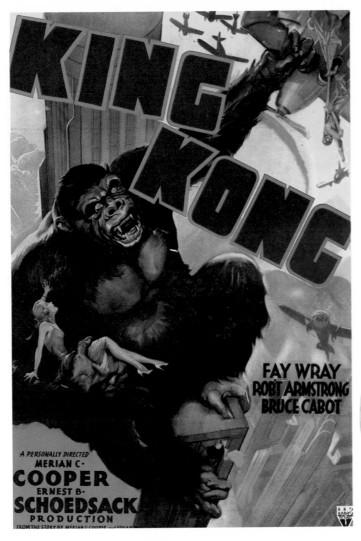

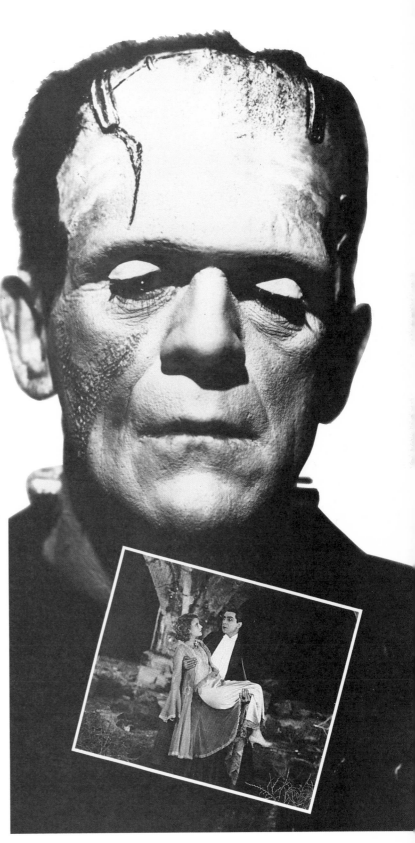

There never was another screamer like Fay Wray **(left)** in **King Kong** (1933); the vampire Count (Bela Lugosi) has a quieter victim (Helen Chandler), **bottom**, on his hands in **Dracula** (1930), while **below** the monster (Boris Karloff) – created by **Frankenstein** (1931).

The films were also some of the most exciting and innovative in the early use of sound with lively dialogue and a vivid aural reproduction of the pulsating excitement of modern urban life. If audiences were stirred by their sense of movement, the moral guardians of the nation were appalled by their tendency to turn outlaws into heroes and to attack social institutions. Hence there was a concerted and successful effort by various influential pressure groups to stamp out those elements in pictures that, to judge from the box-office grosses, the public wanted to see – namely, sex and violence. The result was that Paramount's main asset, Mae West, was sanitized and Warner's resident anarchist, James Cagney, was converted into his own counterpart, a G-Man.

Delight in horror

Universal had great success in the early thirties with its horror films. The vampirism of *Dracula* (1930) did not seem to strike Depression audiences as strange, for the concept of unexpected, unaccountable horror had acquired a contemporary reality. In *Frankenstein* (1931), the monster is a poor creature whose progress and future were at the mercy of forces over which he had no control. Depression audiences found him the most sympathetic character in the film. This was equally true of RKO's *King Kong* (1933): in fact, contemporary audiences were delighted when Kong at one stage launches a ferocious attack on the financial heart of New York.

Above: *A corrupt old senator (Claude Rains) faces an honest young one (James Stewart) in* **Mr. Smith Goes to Washington** *(1939).*

Below: *Halliwell Hobbes, Mischa Auer, Lionel Barrymore in* **You Can't Take It with You** *(1938), Capra's third Oscar in five years.*

However, RKO's big success of the following year, *Little Women*, represents a change of policy and perhaps also a change of national mood. Simple "Americana" films – nostalgic homages to basic American values – were to become something of a speciality at 20th Century-Fox at the end of the decade, notably in films directed by Henry King, like *Alexander's Ragtime Band* (1938).

Columbia's main director of the decade was Frank Capra who made a string of successful social comedies, *It Happened One Night* (1934), *Mr Deeds Goes to Town* (1936), *You Can't Take It with You* (1938) and *Mr Smith Goes to Washington* (1939). All were slick, sentimental, scintillating celebrations of the individual against the system, and of the instinctive wisdom of the ordinary American hero against the worldly corruption and cynicism of the lawyer, the businessman and the politician. They were rich comedies of character in a decade of vintage comic variety. The thirties saw the anarchy of W. C. Fields and the Marx Brothers, the social pathos of Chaplin, the saucy suggestiveness of Mae West, the clowning of Cantor, and the manic inventiveness of screwball comedies like Howard Hawks' *Bringing Up Baby* (1938), which seemed to reflect a vision of the world as maniacal and out of control.

Quality cinema

In the mid-thirties, Warners had a new slogan: "good films – good citizenship". They seemed determined to raise the image of the film industry by tasteful treatments of obviously serious subjects. Their speciality at this time became the screen biography, with Paul Muni mimicking Louis Pasteur in one year, and Emile Zola in the next. The movies extolled enlightenment, progress and rationalism.

Other independent producers were equally committed to what they saw as "quality cinema" – generally speaking, plush but realistic treatments of serious social themes. An important partnership in this regard was that between producer Samuel Goldwyn and director William Wyler. During this period, Wyler directed for Goldwyn *Dodsworth* (1936), a skilful dissection of a disintegrating marriage, based on the novel by Sinclair Lewis; *These Three* (1936), a sentimentalized but still powerful treatment of Lillian Hellman's play *The Children's Hour*, about the destruction of two teachers' lives through rumor and prurience; *Dead End* (1937), a film version of Sidney Kingsley's thesis about the relation between social deprivation and crime; and *Wuthering Heights* (1939), a slimmed-down version of the classic Emily Bronte novel. All of the films were notable for a strong visual and dramatic sense, and a sharp eye for the nuances of class and domestic tensions.

Below: *MGM's Clark Gable and Paramount's Claudette Colbert team up in Columbia's **It Happened One Night** (1934).*

By the end of the thirties, Hollywood seemed to have weathered the worst threats of the decade and come through with some distinction. However, European war was disturbingly on the horizon, and a number of European-born directors, some of whom had recently emigrated to Hollywood, were keen to make films that alerted the American public to the threat of Fascism. It was Dorothy Parker who once remarked, "the only 'ism' Hollywood ever believed in was plagiarism." Not quite true, perhaps: Hollywood has always made a religion of escapism. Despite powerful polemics like Anatole Litvak's *Confessions of a Nazi Spy* (1939), the film industry showed no desire to intervene in the adult ideological debates about Fascism, isolationism and democracy, and audiences clearly preferred the juvenile company of Shirley Temple, Judy Garland and Mickey Rooney.

A peak of achievement

Many commentators have seen 1939 as an especially rich year for Hollywood film. It is a year when a mode of popular and classy film production reached a particular perfection of achievement.

Gone with the Wind established a new level for film melodrama, surpassing in popularity weepies like King Vidor's *Stella Dallas* (1937) for Goldwyn. John Ford's *Stagecoach* set a new standard for the western, unquestionably the most prestigious film of its genre since *Cimarron* (1931). It also gave a first starring role to someone who, until his death forty years later, was to be the most popular of all film actors, John Wayne. Raoul Walsh's *The Roaring Twenties* brought the first decade of the classic Warner Brothers gangster film to a roaring finale, pairing the genre's two brightest stars, Cagney and

Below: *"If I Only Had a Brain", sighs the Scarecrow (Ray Bolger) to Dorothy (Judy Garland) on the Yellow Brick Road in* **The Wizard of Oz** *(1939), directed by Victor Fleming (and King Vidor).*

Bogart, and giving a vivid picture of American society from the aftermath of World War I to the end of Prohibition. Bette Davis suffered more nobly than ever before in Edmund Goulding's *Dark Victory*; Garbo laughed in her last great picture, Lubitsch's *Ninotchka*; Dietrich danced and died in seductive style in *Destry Rides Again*; Charles Laughton's sympathetic monster in *The Hunchback of Notre Dame* rang an unforgettable bell; Robert Donat's schoolmaster in *Goodbye Mr Chips* tugged the heartstrings so effectively that he even stole the Oscar from under the nose of Clark Gable's Rhett Butler; Judy Garland soared over the rainbow in *The Wizard of Oz*; Howard Hawks made arguably his first great picture (if one discounts *Scarface*) in the aviation drama *Only Angels Have Wings*; George Cukor directed the stylish and inimitable *The Women*. Some brilliant writers – Billy Wilder, John Huston, Preston Sturges – were also lurking in the wings, learning the craft, waiting for the moment when they had a chance to direct.

The studio system was at its height in 1939, with close ties between production, distribution and exhibition; when the contract system was at its most powerful; and when writers and directors, except in exceptional cases, were regarded by the studio heads as hired hands. The movies saw themselves as entertainment, not as art. Yet, looking at that far from exhaustive list of outstanding 1939 films, one is hard pressed not to see this as a Golden Age of achievement. Hollywood seemed assured of its audience; seemed almost infallibly shrewd in its importation of talent from the stage or from the Continent; and seemed capable of nurturing its stars from potential to fulfilment with consummate skill. A decade that had begun in widespread doubt and difficulty for the film industry seemed to be ending in a blaze of confidence and prosperity. The decade to come was almost exactly to reverse that progress.

Below: *Francis Lederer in* **Confessions of a Nazi Spy** *(1939).*
Bottom: *An Oklahoma homesteader (Richard Dix) guns down a bad guy (William Collier Jr.) in* **Cimarron** *(1931).*

*A Man and a Woman... Humphrey Bogart and Bette Davis in **Dark Victory** (1939) **(above)**; Noah Beery and Mae West in **She Done* **Him Wrong** *(1933)* **(top right)**; *Melvyn Douglas and Greta Garbo in **Ninotchka** (1939)* **(right)**.

The biggest hits

The Top Ten box-office movies in the USA and Canada between 1930 and 1939 were, in order: Gone with the Wind (1939); Snow White and the Seven Dwarfs (1937); San Francisco (1936); The Kid from Spain (1932); Roman Scandals (1933); 42nd Street (1933); Grand Hotel (1932); I'm No Angel (1933); Little Women (1933); She Done Him Wrong (1933).

The biggest stars

The Top Ten box-office stars between 1932 and 1935 were, in order: Will Rogers; Janet Gaynor; Clark Gable; Marie Dressler; Wallace Beery; Joan Crawford; Shirley Temple; Mae West; Norma Shearer; and, tying for tenth place, Charles Farrell, Eddie Cantor, and Fred Astaire and Ginger Rogers.

And between 1936 and 1940: Clark Gable; Shirley Temple; Mickey Rooney; Spencer Tracy; Astaire and Rogers; Tyrone Power; Sonja Henie; Gary Cooper; Bette Davis; James Cagney.

Drama
GRAND HOTEL (MGM 1932)
Director: Edmund Goulding

"A super-rich pudding" was one critic's description of *Grand Hotel* on its first release. This might be so, but the public has always seemed to like this kind of recipe. Expensive actors and actresses are thrown together in a confined setting. As the stars work out their romantic or financial problems, an audience is permitted the rare privilege of seeming to eavesdrop on an unfamiliar world of wealth, power and glamor. Later films like *Dinner at Eight* (1933), *Weekend at the Waldorf* (1945), *The VIPs* (1963) and *Hotel* (1967) have offered variations on the same formula, with the same expectation of success.

The novelty of *Grand Hotel* was its casting of five major stars – Greta Garbo, John and Lionel Barrymore, Wallace Beery and Joan Crawford – in the leading roles. The theory seemed to be value for money: if an audience comes to see one star, a correspondingly larger audience might flock to see five. The risk is that individual star quality might be diluted and that the film has merely five times as many expensive salaries. Here the gamble paid off. The film was budgeted at $700,000, which included the cost of an impressive art deco set representing the hotel lobby (designed by Alexander Tolubuff and Cedric Gibbons), but it made a profit of nearly a million and was so acclaimed that it received the Best Picture Oscar of 1932.

Intermingled lives
Based on a Vicki Baum play which had failed in Berlin (where it is set) but had been a tremendous success on Broadway, *Grand Hotel* is a human interest drama interweaving the stories of a group of diverse characters who are brought together at key dramatic moments. The range of roles is such that it allows for a wide variety of audience identification. Joan Crawford plays a stenographer who consciously exploits her sex-appeal in a man's world to attain a degree of economic security. Lionel Barrymore wheezes characteristically through his role as an ailing book-keeper who has embezzled some money to spend on a last fling, whilst Wallace Beery plays an industrialist desperately trying to finalize a big deal. Despite the setting, Beery is the only actor in the cast to attempt a German accent. This is essentially a Hollywood hotel. Although aspects of the characters' problems would strike a chord with a Depression audience, the film's basic strategy is to provide glamorous MGM release.

The Baron and the ballerina
The romantic interest is provided by the unexpected love affair which develops between a suicidal Russian ballerina (Greta Garbo) and a phoney Baron (John Barrymore) who is actually a jewel thief. The Baron is described in the play as "fascinatingly handsome, debonair, with a step as elastic as a tennis champion", and although rather old for the part, John Barrymore was preferred over John Gilbert (Garbo's famous partner in her silent films), who had grown morose and downcast at his inability to continue his popularity into the period of the talkies. When asked by cameraman William Daniels how he wanted to look, Barrymore replied: "I'm fifty years old and I want to look like Jackie Cooper's grandson."

In fact, his scenes with Garbo are fascinating particularly because her world-weariness is strikingly more acute than that of a man nearly twice her age. "I want to be alone," Garbo says in this film, the line given some tragic weight by the plight of her character – a *première danseuse* in decline. The Baron rekindles her love of life, and the scenes between Garbo and Barrymore exude the romance and star magic that have always seduced audiences, even in less troubled times.

Grand Hotel is smoothly directed by Edmund Goulding, who was an especially proficient director of actresses, and, although it is not a great movie, it is a work which has continued to symbolize a particularly rich era of screen glamor. It is the film that Jack Lemmon prepares to watch in Billy Wilder's *The Apartment* (1966), as relief from his gloomy surroundings and his sordid situation. It is the essence of movie escapism.

Below: *The life of a typing temp in a hotel has its exciting moments for Flaemmchen (Joan Crawford) when she encounters predatory tycoon Preysing (Wallace Beery): he kills a thief, but his former book-keeper betrays him to the police before sweeping Flaemmchen off to Paris on embezzled money.*

Left: *An unlikely pairing — suicidal ballerina Greta Garbo falls for jewel thief John Barrymore.*

Below: *Barrymore returns her stolen pearls and persuades her to go away with him; alas, his untimely death puts an end to his plan.*

Musical Comedy
THE KID FROM SPAIN (Goldwyn/UA 1932)
Director: Leo McCarey
ROMAN SCANDALS (Goldwyn/UA 1933)
Director: Frank Tuttle

One of the most popular comedians in the early thirties was Eddie Cantor (real name Isidore Itzkowitz). After a successful career in vaudeville and on stage, he had been hired by Paramount at the onset of the sound era to perform in short film comedies, so beginning his movie career. Cantor's stocks-in-trade were his famous rolling eyes, a plaintive voice and an infectious air of reckless enthusiasm. He epitomized the resilient "little American". Unlike Chaplin, he was always victorious over social injustice, an assurance of an optimistic outcome that undoubtedly endeared him to the public. Indeed, his persona of the sensitive, jittery innocent has some similarities to that of Woody Allen in his early comedies.

Cantor's two greatest film successes were for producer Sam Goldwyn, who was a great admirer of Cantor. In *The Kid from Spain*, on the run from the police in Mexico, he has to pose as a Spanish bullfighter, which leads to a hilarious yet convincing bullfight sequence. In *Roman Scandals* (1933), Cantor dreams himself back into ancient Rome from Depression America.

The popularity of these films was not simply due to the presence of Cantor himself. For one thing, both films were lavishly mounted. They featured the famous Goldwyn girls (Betty Grable and Paulette Goddard can be glimpsed in one of the numbers of *The Kid from Spain*), and the plots were punctuated by dazzlingly choreographed routines by Busby Berkeley, which lifted the films onto a new plane of imagination.

Also, in these films, Cantor was undoubtedly well served and supported by expert craftsmanship. For example, *The Kid from Spain* was photographed by Gregg Toland, who was later to win an Oscar for *Wuthering Heights* (1939) and break

Below: *The Kid from Spain* *featured Eddie Cantor* (**inset**) *and the Goldwyn Girls, who included Betty Grable, Paulette Goddard (and, later, in **Roman Scandals**, Lucille Ball).*

"We'll be glad when you're dead, you rascal, you!" is the heated reply to Eddie Cantor's *"Keep Young and Beautiful"* in **Roman Scandals**.

new ground with his astounding deep-focus effects in Orson Welles' *Citizen Kane* (1941). It was directed by the extremely talented Leo McCarey who, on the strength of it and to his subsequent regret, was to be invited by the Marx Brothers to direct their next feature, *Duck Soup* (1933). McCarey's greatest success was to come in the following decade with *Going My Way* (1944). So the film had a lot of merit and skill to entrance an audience quite apart from the particular appeal of Cantor. Similarly with *Roman Scandals*, which had a story by two redoubtable writers, George S. Kaufman and Robert E. Sherwood, and did so well probably because it was the best film vehicle Cantor ever had.

Scandals and solutions

As well as having some splendid musical numbers, the film delighted audiences with its anachronistic jokes about ancient Rome which were simultaneously jokes about popular Hollywood epics such as *Ben-Hur* (1925) that had so enthralled the public in the previous decade. As well as alluding to the famous set-piece of *Ben-Hur*, which is fixed in the minds of all movie fans, the exciting chariot race finale anticipates the similar ending of *A Funny Thing Happened on the Way to the Forum* by thirty years.

Cantor's dream about ancient Rome is not only a comic formula – a man dreams himself into another age – that will be used in other popular comedies like the Bing Crosby vehicle, *A Connecticut Yankee in King Arthur's Court* (1949). It releases him temporarily from some of the worries of the Depression, which is probably how it was intended to affect audiences too. However, in the modern story, Cantor, fortified by his Roman experience, returns to save some poor people from being evicted from their homes by a ruthless businessman. In blending ancient and modern, Cantor's film also cunningly blended escapism and wish-fulfilment. You can not only escape from your problems: what you learn from that escape might also help you solve them.

During the late thirties, Cantor's "little man" characterizations were progressively upstaged by the return of Chaplin in full flight in *Modern Times* (1936), and by the more sophisticated comic morality plays of Frank Capra mentioned above. But Cantor's contribution to the cinema was recognized by a film about his life, *The Eddie Cantor Story* (1953), and an honorary Oscar in 1956 "for distinguished service to the film industry". His most distinguished service was undoubtedly his success at cheering up audiences at a time when they needed it.

Musical
42nd STREET (WB 1933)
Director: Lloyd Bacon

Choreographer Busby Berkeley was a key figure in various phases of the thirties musical. In the space of slightly over a year (1932-33), he worked as dance director on four of the top hits of the decade – *42nd Street, Footlight Parade, The Kid from Spain* and *Roman Scandals*. Berkeley remained at Warners until 1938, having graduated from choreographer to full director status, and, in 1939, he joined Arthur Freed's new musical unit at MGM.

When Berkeley had first arrived at Warners in 1932, the movie musical had been all but killed off by the large number of static and unimaginative stage adaptations. In *42nd Street*, in numbers such as "Young and Healthy", "Shuffle Off to Buffalo" and the title number, Berkeley developed his unique style of elaborate filmic choreography by making use of kaleidoscopic patterns of dancers captured from extremely high or low angles, or from a moving camera.

Berkeley's success was based on his ability to visualize even the most elaborate and complex sequences in advance. "I never needed retakes," he said. "I would plan it all so carefully in my mind, and I worked out every single camera set up." Acknowledging the help he obtained from outstanding designers and writers, Berkeley said he thought the appeal of his work came from his ability to create spectacle from a parade of gorgeous girls. "It is not the story, it is not the stars, not the music," he said. "What people want to see are beautiful girls."

Spirit of the age
This might be partly true, but it is not wholly true of *42nd Street*, where the story and the cast are all important. On the surface, the film is the most fantasized of backstage musicals. A young understudy (Ruby Keeler) gets her big break when the star breaks her ankle, and, going out a youngster, she comes back a star. But *42nd Street* is also a document of the period, a "New Deal" musical which undoubtedly caught the spirit of a particular era.

Like many Warner Brothers musicals of the decade (and unlike those made at Paramount and those subsequently to be made at MGM), *42nd Street* is characterized by its realism. The routine slog of theatrical life is vividly caught, as is the rivalry and ribaldry of working-class girls in a tough profession. The understudy's success is the result not really of luck but of hard work. She is helped to success by the obsession and dedication of her director (a brilliant performance from Warner Baxter), who has to fight personal exhaustion and depression to bring the show to a triumphant conclusion.

A cure for the Depression
Success is a combination of team effort and enlightened guidance. In that respect, and given its gritty realism, *42nd Street* is not just a lively musical, but a hopeful message for the times. All credit to the magnificent monochrome photography of Sol Polito, Jack Okey's startling art direction, Harry Warren and Al Dubin's delightful score, Lloyd Bacon's driving direction, and to those Berkeley routines which, in both their intimate and dazzling moments, foreshadow the possibilities

Above: *Producer Julian Marsh (Warren Baxter) threatens big trouble when musical star Dorothy Brock (Bebe Daniels) injures her ankle; but good little Peggy Sawyer (Ruby Keeler) is standing by, ready to save the day – or rather first night. Though initially* (**inset**) *he was not too crazy about her work ("can't sing, can dance a little"?), and even "Anytime Annie" (Ginger Rogers – center right) looked scathing – Peggy eventually obeys his injunction, "Sawyer, you're going out there a youngster but you've got to come back a star!" Her dream was realized thanks very largely to Busby Berkeley's all-out title number* (**right**).

of film ballet that Fred Astaire and Gene Kelly were to explore in future years. But, reading the reviews of the time, one is struck by the impact made on the critics by the film's seeming authenticity. Said *Picturegoer*: "It is its *authentic* atmosphere, fine detail and strong human power ... that lift this picture from the conventional ..." *Variety* claimed that "everything about the production *rings true* ..." "There was a time," said *The New York Times*, "when spectators were satiated with backstage stuff, but here it is pictured brightly and with a degree of authenticity that makes it diverting." Nominated for an Oscar as Best Picture, *42nd Street* was not only a cure for the blues: it seemed to drive away the Depression through its energy, enterprise and effort.

Comedy
SHE DONE HIM WRONG (Paramount 1933)
Director: Lowell Sherman
I'M NO ANGEL (Paramount 1933)
Director: Wesley Ruggles

"I used to be Snow White – but I drifted." So said Mae West, one of the most provocative comediennes of the screen and widely described at the time as America's Statue of Sexual Liberty. In the movies of the early thirties, she did for sex what Cagney did for crime: that is, made it dangerously attractive. In 1933, two low-budget comedies of hers not only made her the biggest box-office draw of the year but are often credited with saving Paramount Studios from bankruptcy.

However, Hollywood had been under pressure for some time by various groups who criticized the motion picture industry for glamorizing crime and displaying overt sexuality. A cautionary book by Henry J. Forman, *Our Movie-Made Children* (1933), attacked permissive cinema for the effect it was having on the youth of America. The appearance of Mae West merely fanned the fires of moralistic dismay. Symbol of

Below: *Diamond Lil (Mae West) resists the advances of a boorish suitor (Owen Moore) in* **She Done Him Wrong.**

cinematic virtue Mary Pickford was quoted at the time as saying: "I passed the door of my young niece's room … and I heard her singing that song from *Diamond Lil* – I say 'that song' just because I'd blush to quote the title even here." (For the record, "that song" was entitled "A Guy What Takes His Time".) After the formation of the National Legion of Decency in 1933, which advised customers what films to boycott on grounds of "immorality", the studios had no option but to take heed. The scripts of Mae West's future films were diluted and her appeal inevitably diminished.

A woman without illusions

Mae West was forty when she made her screen debut. Along with W. C. Fields and the Marx Brothers she was an early comic subversive of the sound era. Her speciality was husky-voiced invitation behind an exceptionally alluring figure that was emphasized by tight-fitting, slinky dresses and often adorned by flashy jewelry. The male audience responded to her as a blatant sex symbol, knowing, experienced, and, for all her superior quips, flatteringly acknowledging that men were the most important things in her world. But women also liked her for her confidence, her wit, her relaxed style of delivery, and her satirically contemptuous attitude to male lust, which seemed to seize the sexual initiative away from the male to the female. "Am I making myself clear, boys?" she says in come-hither fashion in *I'm No Angel*, before murmuring under her breath: "Suckers."

In *She Done Him Wrong* (based on her own hit play, *Diamond Lil*), she plays a saloon keeper attracted to a missionary who is actually an undercover policeman, a part played by one of her protégés, Cary Grant. In *I'm No Angel*, she plays a carnival dancer who is let off a murder charge and who moves into high society. The films are short (in both cases, less than eighty minutes) and also cheap, because the settings are relatively restricted. The jolly evocation of period no doubt contributed to the films' appeal because they inspired a nostalgia for simpler, happier times.

"Haven't you ever met a man who could make you happy?" asks Cary Grant in *She Done Him Wrong*. "Sure," replies Mae West, before adding impishly, "lots of times." Later Grant asks if she minds his holding her hand, to which she replies, firmly: "It ain't heavy, I can hold it myself." It was this kind of impudence and independence that audiences relished. Here was a woman who had no inhibitions about sex but also no illusions about romance: for a moment, this combination seemed a healthy and liberating alternative to the usual film formula that extolled primness and patriarchy as the prime social and sexual virtues.

A puritan backlash was probably inevitable, but while the permissive era lasted, Mae West was the undisputed queen of comic innuendo and sexual equality. Examples of her influence and legacy might include Marlene Dietrich in *Destry Rides Again* (1939), Madeline Kahn in *Blazing Saddles* (1973), Bette Midler and Joan Rivers.

Disaster Movie

SAN FRANCISCO (MGM 1936)
Director: W. S. Van Dyke

"This is *my* idea of a prestige picture," said MGM boss Louis B. Mayer of *San Francisco*. What Mayer meant by "prestige picture" was not a probing analysis of social problems or a work of artistic profundity, but a glossy extrovert entertainment that made him a lot of money. *San Francisco* qualifies on that score. Shot in fifty-two days at a cost of $1.3 million, it made a profit of nearly twice that amount at the box-office.

Nevertheless, the film was no ordinary commercial package: an aura of prestige clings lightly to it. It was co-written by Anita Loos, best known as the authoress of the classic comic novel, *Gentlemen Prefer Blondes* (1925) and of MGM scripts like *Red-Headed Woman* (1932) and *Saratoga* (1937) that were carefully tailored to the liberated temperament and talents of blonde bombshell Jean Harlow. With *San Francisco*, Ms Loos and her writing partner Robert Hopkins conceived the script as a tribute to the city they had both known in their youth; and also as a tribute to the gambler Wilson Mizner who had run a San Francisco gambling house and who had been a close friend of Anita Loos until his death in 1933.

A final spur to achieve the utmost excellence in the script was the death, before the film went into production, of studio chief Irving Thalberg, to whom Loos had been devoted. The plot concerns the on-off romance between a gruff, good-natured saloon owner, Blackie Norton (Clark Gable), and a night club singer (Jeanette MacDonald) with ambitions to be an opera star. The conflict is put into perspective by the eruption of an earthquake.

The film had its troubles during production. There were objections to a scene where Blackie socks his best friend, a priest (Spencer Tracy), on the jaw, so the scene had to be reworked for Tracy to appear the moral victor. Anita Loos was not absolutely happy with the choice of W. S. "Woody" Van Dyke as director, who seemed to her to be stronger on action and speed than on character and charm. Van Dyke she said, "was capable of understanding the mentality of South Sea savages but was an oaf when it came to the subtleties of the San Francisco tenderloin."

Shattering spectacles

Subtlety and tenderness are certainly not qualities that one prizes in *San Francisco*, but, characteristically, Van Dyke gives the film tremendous pace, driving it hectically forward, even through the musical numbers, which otherwise might have slowed things down. Gable's rough-diamond performance is a fascinating anticipation of his portrayal of Rhett Butler in *Gone with the Wind*, just as his rather uneasy relationship with the girl anticipates the Butler-Scarlett O'Hara relationship.

As with all disaster movies, however, it is the disaster itself that counts. The recreation of the 1906 San Francisco earthquake (special visual effects courtesy of Arnold Gillespie and James Basevi and Oscar-winning sound effects by Douglas Shearer) looks spectacular even today. The film's success spawned other disaster movies, such as MGM's *The Good Earth* (1936) with its ferocious locust attack, and John Ford's *The Hurricane* (1937).

Many theories have been put forward for the success of disaster movies, particularly at certain times in movie history. They certainly show off the cinema's capacity for spectacle, but they also seem mysteriously to give the public solace during times of trouble. The physical collapse of society corresponds to an audience's sense of a world in chaos, but audiences also take heart from the capacity of the people in the film to endure and reconstruct something from the rubble.

With its blazingly religious finale to the tune of "Battle Hymn of the Republic", *San Francisco* is a pugnacious affirmation of the ability of human beings to rise above any disaster, be it natural or economic. If we can survive an earthquake, it seems to say, we can certainly survive a Depression. Behind it is the spirit implicit in President Roosevelt's words: "We have nothing to fear but fear itself." The disaster movie was to come into vogue again during the seventies, when the economies and stability of the Western world seemed under threat. In characterization, special effects and even uplifting songs, *San Francisco* was to provide an important model.

Above: *Club owner Blackie Norton (Clark Gable) is a gambling man who takes a heavy loss when his Barbary Coast joint is burned down in dubious circumstances.*

Right: *The love of Blackie's life is a touring opera singer (Jeanette MacDonald). She appears for a while at his Barbary Coast nightspot though her real love is singing arias from "Faust" and "La Traviata". Her best numbers are the romantic "Would You?" (reprised in* **Singin' in the Rain** *– 1952) and the rousing "San Francisco (Open Your Golden Gate)", which has virtually become the signature tune of the West Coast's most elegant metropolis.*

Comedy
MODERN TIMES (UA 1936)
Director: Charles Chaplin

Modern Times was Charles Chaplin's last non-talking film and his last to feature the Tramp. There had been a tremendous amount of interest and advance speculation

Right: *The Tramp (Chaplin) and the Gamin (sic) (Paulette Goddard) walk off at the end, not into the sunset but into the uncertainty of a new life.*

about the film before it arrived, so it was perhaps inevitable that the critical and audience response to the film seemed at the time somewhat muted, especially after the enormous acclaim for Chaplin's previous film *City Lights* (1931). Nevertheless, it was still one of the most lucrative films of the decade and has remained a classic of screen comedy.

Chaplin stated his intention in the film as follows: "I wanted to say something about the way life is being standardized and channelized, and men turned into machines." This observation of the mechanization of man provides much of the humor of the opening part of the film. A

shot of a flock of sheep with one black sheep (implicitly, Chaplin himself) is followed by a shot of men going sheep-like into work. Charlie's job of tightening nuts on an assembly line is so repetitive that he is still twitching when the machine stops, and he later mistakes the buttons on a secretary's dress for the nuts on the machine. Used as a guinea pig for a feeding machine that has been designed to eliminate the lunch-hour, Charlie is attacked by his food when the machine gets out of control. Small wonder that his industrial experience is to drive Charlie to a nervous breakdown.

After this brilliantly comic evocation of assembly-line existence, Chaplin now sets about creating a vivid, funny but also disturbing picture of life as experienced by the insulted, injured and unemployed of Depression America. There are some funny routines when he inadvertently leads a Communist march and foils a prison escape, but there are also serious moments, when, for example, the police open fire on the unemployed, and theft is seen as a justifiable response to poverty. At one stage, Charlie would prefer to stay in prison rather than be released and have to face the world outside. *Modern Times* was the film that particularly marked Chaplin's increasing sense of the social responsibility of the film-maker. His criticism of injustice and his indictment of brutal and materialist political philosophies were to be carried even further in *The Great Dictator* (1940) and *Monsieur Verdoux* (1947).

Sugaring the pill

Chaplin's genius was his ability to sugar quite radical ideas about society with inventive comic routines that are as hilarious in execution as they are sometimes horrifying in implication. In *Modern Times*, in his search for the basics of life to survive – love, food and money – Charlie has to wait on tables and improvise a garbled nonsense song to earn his keep. At one stage, in a deserted department store, he skates blindfold towards an abyss, which might well be a metaphor for Chaplin's vision of man's journey through life. Dickensian sentimentality and social incisiveness are married to an eloquent gift for pantomime that unites pathos and profundity.

Some critics complained about Chaplin's continued disdain for sound and his use of titles in *Modern Times*, and some thought his view of modern industrial society old-fashioned and romantically pessimistic. But the horrors of depersonalization in a technological society are still with us. One could argue that the Tramp's attempted solution to being terrorized by a system, far from being old-fashioned, anticipated the activities of the drop-outs and disaffected youth of the 1960s: that is, find a mate (vivaciously played here by Paulette Goddard) and opt out of society altogether, with its spoonfeeding of mechanized responses. As Graham Greene said of Chaplin's ideas about society: "They are not enough for a reformer, but they have proved amply sufficient for an artist."

Below: *The disturbing if comic events in an assembly-line factory as Charlie gets caught up in the poetic dance of the machinery but miraculously survives. W. C. Fields used to say (disparagingly) that Chaplin was really a ballet dancer.*

Literary Adaptation
LITTLE WOMEN (RKO 1933)
Director: George Cukor

If producer David O. Selznick brought a literary classic to the screen, one thing was certain: he would stay faithful to his source material. In one of his memos, he records with horror that, when he scheduled *Little Women* for production, the heads of the RKO circuit suggested that he should modernize it. Selznick refused to do any such thing, and the film's success revived an interest in costume drama.

A version of *Little Women* had originally been made in 1919. According to the associate producer of the 1933 version, Kenneth MacGowan, the decision to remake it was a response to the modest success of *Rebecca of Sunnybrook Farm* (1932) and an order from his RKO boss to find a "sweetness and light" story. Louisa May Alcott's novel about a New England family during the time of the Civil War seemed to fit the bill admirably. Katharine Hepburn was cast as the tomboy, Jo, and her sisters were played by Joan Bennett (Amy), Frances Dee (Meg) and Jean Parker (Beth).

Traditions upheld
The choice of director proved crucial. George Cukor has admitted that, when he was asked to do it, he had not read the novel. When he did, he said: "I was absolutely startled because it had all the American virtues – duty, love of family, respect for parents, hard work, all the staples that I think are admirable."

Possibly because of the enormous and revelatory impact on him by the novel, Cukor projected those qualities with great purity and power, and there is no doubt that national audiences found this reaffirmation of traditional American values immensely moving as well as reassuring in a time of social turmoil.

The danger with the material, Cukor thought, was sentimentality, particularly in such events as the death of the little sister and the later introduction of a romantic hero. But Cukor was as insistent as Selznick on fidelity to the text. If you adapt a talented novel, he felt, you do not try to "slick it up" but understand and include its weaknesses as well as strengths, which are equally part of the tone and essence of the work.

The performances greatly added to the conviction, particularly that of Katharine Hepburn, in one of the greatest of her thirties characterizations as a heroine looking to fulfil herself outside the conventional wife-mother role allotted to women. "Kate had come from a large New England family like the one in the story and identified with the novel's spirit," said Cukor. "She cast a magic spell over the entire production."

Perhaps because the film is co-scripted by a woman, Sarah Y. Mason, the feelings of the characters seem very authentic and believable. (Nearly all of Cukor's films of the decade included a female writer on the screenplay credits, which no doubt partly accounts for the sympathetic portrayal of women in his films and his reputation as a "woman's director".) The authenticity is enhanced by skilful art direction by Van Nest Polglase and Hobe Erwin, who went to considerable lengths to reproduce the feeling of nineteenth-century New England.

Above: *Jo (Katharine Hepburn) enjoys the New England winter with a friendly snowman.*

Good taste pays off
In fact, this interpretation of *Little Women* (more so than the later 1949 version) seems to have worked because, rather than attempting to sentimentalize the original, everyone sought their own truth in the material. For Cukor, it was a repository of the most desirable American values. For Katharine Hepburn, it was a reminder of the values of her own family and a statement about the different roles and potentialities of women in society. For audiences, it hearteningly evoked a simpler, more innocent and optimistic world. For the industry, when the movies were coming increasingly under pressure from censors and civic guardians of public decency to offer more wholesome entertainment, *Little Women* came like a breath of fresh air. It could not have been further away from Mae West, it cleaned up at the box-office, and it was nominated for a Best Film Oscar. To Hollywood's relief, merit and morality once again meant money.

Right: *Sparks fly between Jo and Amy across the sketch pads.*

Below right: *The four March sisters are (from left to right) Meg (Frances Dee), Amy (Joan Bennett), Beth (Jean Parker) and Jo.*

35

Fantasy
SNOW WHITE AND THE SEVEN DWARFS
(Disney/RKO 1937)

Nowadays Walt Disney's name is synonymous with simple, wholesome, safe family entertainment. So it is a little surprising to turn up reviews in the thirties and find Disney being discussed as an artist on a par with Chaplin and Capra, as an independent talent who loved movies, broke taboos, and was applauded for his daring by audiences and critics alike. Between 1932 and 1939 he won an Oscar every year.

Based on a fairy tale by the brothers Grimm, *Snow White* was his biggest gamble to date. It was the first full-length Disney cartoon; took three years to make at a cost of a million-and-a-half dollars; utilized the skills of 570 artists and made use of 250,000 drawings. It turned out to be a huge success, the biggest grossing movie since D. W. Griffith's *Birth of a Nation*.

Part of the attraction was unquestionably the film's novelty. But Disney had a shrewd commercial mind. In addition to the novelty, there are a lot of familiar popular ingredients, colorfully mixed. There is excitement, as in Snow White's vivid flight through the forest from the Wicked Queen who is trying to have her killed (the best Disney cartoons always have their quota of suspense, which is every bit as important as the sentiment). Humor is delightfully integrated, as in the house-cleaning sequence, where squirrels use their tails as brushes and birds fly with sheets to shake them dry. Also the music is skilfully used, with an appropriate thematic motif for each of the main characters and a tuneful score that features such endearing and enduringly popular songs as "Some Day My Prince Will Come", "With a Smile and a Song" and "Whistle While You Work".

Fun, fear and fantasy

In later years, Disney productions were to go a little sentimental, and there is a trace of that in the episodes involving Snow White and the Prince. Mainly, at this stage of his development, Disney's cartoons offered fantasy, fun and fear in more or less equal proportions. In *Snow White* Disney's feeling for nature is shown in the evocation of green woodlands and attractive earthy textures. More importantly, his films have a feeling for human nature. The evil of the Wicked Queen has a frightening intensity – as piercing as the bright red of her poisoned apple. It is the kind of thing that would stand out in a child's nightmares, and an adult audience of the thirties would also not have to think hard for modern parallels to this vision of undiluted evil.

Like Chaplin, Disney was a law unto himself: a one-man cinematic institution. He was his own author, director and counsel. Just as Chaplin showed that silence could still be eloquent in the sound era, Disney showed that he could bring as much humor and humanity into a drawing as most actors could achieve in a full-blown characterization.

The film's artful combination of color, fantasy, song and sweetness had its influence on the cinema of its day. MGM was encouraged to embark on *The Wizard of Oz* (1939); 20th Century-Fox put Shirley Temple into her first color feature, *The Little Princess* (1938); and Alexander Korda and Michael Powell began preparation on the first British fantasy film in color, *The Thief of Bagdad* (1940). *Snow White* is probably the ultimate Disney achievement, with a monetary spin-off from the sale of toys, books and records, in addition to the gross of the film itself, that was to influence the future merchandizing of film. In terms of his Peter Pan-like ability to enter into the mind of a child, Disney has only been matched

Below: *Disney's magnificent creation, the Wicked Queen, hatches a plot to kill the too beautiful Snow White.*

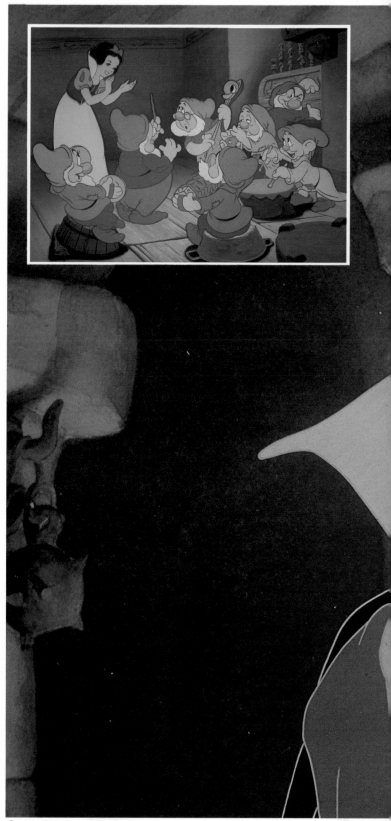

in modern times by Steven Spielberg. In Spielberg's production *Gremlins* (1984), the fiendish creatures of the title break into a cinema and start projecting *Snow White*. Although hell bent on mischief, they are nevertheless absolutely charmed by the movie. Audiences, however diverse, always have been.

Left inset: *After dinner entertainment by the dwarfs, while* **right** *Dopey asks for a special kiss.*

Adventure
THE ADVENTURES OF ROBIN HOOD
(WB 1938)
Directors: Michael Curtiz, William Keighley

In 1938, Warner Brothers decided to remake one of Douglas Fairbanks's silent classics, *Robin Hood* (1922). It proved to be a timely and inspired decision. Since the Fairbanks film, the screen had acquired sound: this could give added fury and excitement to the sword duels, and provide the added dimension of the rapier-like quips.

Equally importantly, the cinema had acquired color, without quite knowing what to do with it. The first Technicolor feature, Rouben Mamoulian's *Becky Sharp* (1935), based on a stage version of Thackeray's novel *Vanity Fair*, was rather stylized and studio-bound for audiences' tastes. Henry Hathaway's *The Trail of the Lonesome Pine* (1936) was much more successful, for the location shooting allowed the camera to catch the color of natural landscapes more vividly than ever before. The first big live-action Technicolor hits were *The Adventures of Robin Hood* and *The Trail of the Lonesome Pine*. In keeping with its reputation as the most pioneering of Hollywood studios, Warners had made a serious attempt to upgrade the quality of its color productions, recognizing that the adventure film has always appealed primarily to the senses and that color might provide that extra intoxicating ingredient.

Also Warners had found in Errol Flynn the swashbuckling successor to Fairbanks. At one time Flynn had been intended by the studio as their answer to Clark Gable. However, Warners quickly appreciated that Flynn as an actor lacked Gable's dramatic range (Bette Davis has said she audibly sighed at Flynn's attempt to simulate nobility in their 1939 film together, *The Private Lives of Elizabeth and Essex*). But, as Jack Warner said about him, "Actor or no actor, Flynn showered an audience with sparks when he laughed, when he fought or when he loved. He made people feel young and alive."

He was never more perfectly cast than as Robin Hood, whether jauntily striding into a castle with a deer on his shoulders or trading insults as well as sword wounds with the villainous Guy of Gisbourne (Basil Rathbone).

Flair and fervour

In *Robin Hood*, Flynn is given the support of Warners' splendid repertory of acting talent: Olivia de Havilland as a winsome Maid Marian; Eugene Pallette as a prodigious Friar Tuck ("One of us!" says one of the Merry Men about Tuck, "He looks like three of us!"); Alan Hale as the heartiest of Little Johns; and Claude Rains as the most cunning of King Johns. The action is dashingly driven along by what is perhaps Erich Wolfgang Korngold's finest score (an unforgettable splash of orchestral revelry, vividly matched to the action, during Robin's ambush on Sir Guy's men in the forest); and by every facet of studio craftsmanship, in which the gleaming photography of Sol Polito and Tony Gaudio stands out. It has a quality of innocence that marks the best adventures, appealing to an audience's sense of a world of idealized excitement, in which compelling vice (ranging from surly villainy to deceptively suave low cunning) is finally and inevitably vanquished by an even more fascinating and thrilling virtue.

The gallant Robin (Errol Flynn) with, **above,** *jolly Friar Tuck (Eugene Pallette) in Sherwood Forest,* **right** *Maid Marian (Olivia de Havilland); and* **inset right** *at Nottingham Castle fighting it out with Sir Guy of Gisbourne (Basil Rathbone).*

Given the high spirits of the film, it is perhaps surprising to remember that it had its share of troubles during production. The original director, William Keighley, was fired after seven weeks, apparently for setting too languid a tempo and for appearing to send up the material. Flynn was none too keen on Michael Curtiz as replacement (on the 1935 *Captain Blood*, Flynn claimed that Curtiz was so bloodthirsty that he had insisted the tips be taken off the swords), but there were few directors around who could excel Curtiz for pace and excitement. The film was also expensive, which meant finally that its profit margin was relatively small. But it deserves inclusion here because of the number of people who saw it, for the frequency of its revivals, and for its enduring popularity. Even in a period of classic adventure films – one thinks also of Selznick's production of *The Prisoner of Zenda* (1937) and George Stevens' *Gunga Din* (1939) – *The Adventures of Robin Hood* remains the most memorable – for its flair, its fervour and for Flynn.

Melodrama
GONE WITH THE WIND (Selznick/MGM 1939)
Director: Victor Fleming

Above: *Love on a grand scale. Scarlett O'Hara (Vivien Leigh), already twice married, is stuck in her stubborn adolescent crush for high-principled Ashley Wilkes (Leslie Howard), who runs her husband's lumber business. He half-reluctantly responds to her youth and beauty, remaining faithful to his wife, Melanie.*

In an early scene of Billy Wilder's *Sunset Boulevard* (1950), a screenwriter is having a furious argument with the studio reader, who has dismissed his script as "flat and trite". "You'd have turned down *Gone with the Wind!*" storms the writer. "No, that was me," says a disconsolate Paramount producer, who has been listening to the row. "I said – who wants to see another Civil War picture?"

In the hands of producer David O. Selznick, *Gone with the Wind* became anything but "another Civil War picture". For one thing, the war is relegated to the background, there are no battle scenes, and even the issue of Negro slavery scarcely raises its head. Selznick's interest was in creating a great romantic melodrama, which would in effect unite North and South, male and female, in lamenting the loss of a genteel society and in following with rapture the fluctuating fortunes of a passionate relationship. He set about this job with a publicist's zeal. An immense amount of interest was generated about the film before it had even been screened, partly through Selznick's no-expense-spared attempt to duplicate the book's popularity (he had bought the rights before it had proved so successful) but mainly through his launching of a massive campaign to find the right actress to play Scarlett O'Hara, a campaign that had still not been concluded when the film started shooting.

Some of the unsuccessful contenders were to be given starring vehicles by their own studios as a sort of compensation, like, for example, Bette Davis in *Dark Victory* and *The Private Lives of Elizabeth and Essex*, and Norma Shearer, Joan Crawford, Paulette Goddard and Joan Fontaine in George Cukor's *The Women* (1939). Cukor himself had started directing *Gone with the Wind*, but had been replaced by Victor Fleming, reputedly on the insistence of Clark Gable who felt Cukor's reputation as a "woman's director" might lead to his own role being undermined.

The widely publicized search for an actress to play Scarlett has had a special fascination for writers on Hollywood (most recently in Garson Kanin's novel, *Moviola*). The casting of Vivien Leigh took most observers by surprise. Laurence Olivier had wanted Vivien Leigh to play Cathy in William Wyler's film of *Wuthering Heights* (Wyler had offered her the secondary part of Isabella, saying: "You're totally unknown in America and you won't get anything better for your first Hollywood part!"). Whilst visiting Olivier during the filming of *Wuthering Heights*, Miss Leigh was recommended to Selznick, and the rest is both history and legend.

Ingredients for success
What of the attraction of the film itself? It is a love story on a grand scale – at that time, one of the longest feature films in screen history. It had elements of *The Taming of the Shrew* (tough hero tries to tame rebellious heroine), *Antony and Cleopatra* (a tragic love story), and *War and Peace* (love fighting for survival against massive social turmoil). The setting of the American South seemed peculiarly right for the outsized emotions and anticipated a whole train of massive Southern melodramas, from Tennessee Williams to *Dallas*. The film has spectacle (that memorable tracking shot of the war wounded, the burning of Atlanta); it has controversy (would the film get away with Butler's profanity – "Frankly, my dear, I don't give a damn" – and his angry carrying off of Scarlett to their marriage bed?); most of all it has the tension of a romantic story with an uncertain outcome. Would Scarlett see through the self-absorbed gentility of Ashley Wilkes (Leslie Howard) and accept the love of Rhett Butler (Clark Gable)? It is not a subtle dilemma, but part of the film's power comes from its polarity of extremes – the weak (Wilkes) against the strong (Butler), the good (Melanie) against the scheming (Scarlett), the quintessence of feminine caprice (Scarlett) brought into riveting conflict with the archetype of sturdy masculinity (Rhett).

The casting turned out to be fine, Gable justifying the public's choice of him as Butler, and Vivien Leigh suggesting a sharp intelligence beneath the feminine guile. The emotions are heightened by a spanking Max Steiner score. "Tara's Theme" gives a unity to the film's structure, poignantly reminding an audience of a former world of stability and continuity, and having an unbridled romanticism that instantly involves a spectator in the film's emotional sweep. Not until Maurice Jarre's "Lara's Theme" in *Doctor Zhivago* was there a theme tune for an epic film that so instantly captured public attention.

The end of an era
Premiered in December 1939, *Gone with the Wind* went on to win nine Academy Awards. It represented the true end of an era, the ultimate thirties film in style and conception. It was big, brash and romantic. It was star-studded and spectacular, sure of its audience appeal, and spoke more to the heart than to the mind. It had a massive narrative authority, and put less store on personal expression than on mass emotion. It is the ultimate studio film, and the vindication of the studio system, a monument of popular art and Hollywood craftsmanship. As a lament for a vanishing world, the film contained its own implicit comment on both the coming war and on Hollywood itself. The film capital was never to look quite so self-confident again.

Left: *This glamorous publicity shot of Vivien Leigh reveals both the elaborate production values of the film (established by designer William Cameron Menzies) and the striking Technicolor photography (by Ernest Haller).*

Below: *Scarlett caught up with Rhett Butler (Clark Gable) in the defeat of the South, symbolized by the burning of Atlanta, and the decline of Tara, the O'Hara's beloved family mansion.*

CHAPTER TWO:

THE FORTIES

Aboom in film production began in the early forties and rapidly reached its peak during the years 1943 to 1946. However, the essentially fragile nature of the boom was soon exposed with the end of wartime austerity. Film had been the leading form of entertainment for millions during the war, but as soon as cars and houses became available again, there was more competition for people's money. People were soon looking for new and more exciting ways to spend their leisure time, no longer dependent for their entertainment on the local movie theater.

The forties period was the apex of studio film-making in America, but the decline in audiences was apparent by the end of the decade. Not only that, but the "consent decrees" of 1948 forced the production companies to sell off their theater chains. This severed the close links between production and exhibition which had guaranteed a market for their pictures. The dismantling of the studio system had begun.

Profits at their peak

The wartime boom itself had been full of paradoxes. With various restrictions and shortages, and with many of the top directors, stars and other key personnel away in the armed services, there was a serious decline in film production from the major companies (from an average of 370 per year from 1938 to 1942 to 280 during 1943-4 and 245 per year from 1945 to 1947).

The result was that the peak years of moviegoing – there were, for example, 4,000 million tickets sold in America in 1946 – coincided with a fall in the total number of new pictures. However, this also meant an increase in the profitability of individual pictures and a jump in profits for the film companies. At the end of the war, too, there was an enormous demand for the backlog of Hollywood movies that had been suppressed during the war in Nazi-occupied Europe. For a while Hollywood seemed to have complete dominance over the international market.

The range of hit films was as wide as ever. Hollywood had by now come to terms with color and used it lavishly on its escapist entertainment. Sumptuous costume dramas like *Forever Amber* (1947) and *The Three Musketeers* (1948) found a large audience. A ballet film, Powell and Pressburger's *The Red Shoes* (1948), also scored an unexpected success, the most lucrative of the movies that represented

Top: *Frank Sinatra and Gene Kelly in* **Anchors Aweigh** *(1944), produced by Joe Pasternak.*

Above: *Returned veteran Dana Andrews and sluttish wife Virginia Mayo in* **The Best Years of Our Lives** *(1946).*

Right: *Fred Astaire and Judy Garland are "A Couple of Swells" (song by Irving Berlin) in* **Easter Parade** *(1948).*

The Red Shoes (1948). **Above:** *Betty Hutton as Annie Oakley and Howard Keel as a rival shot in* **Annie Get Your Gun** *(1950).*

the postwar British cinema renaissance. At Paramount, Cecil B. DeMille continued his winning ways with *Reap the Wild Wind* (1942), which is most famous for its climactic fight with a giant squid, and *Unconquered* (1947), which *Time* magazine succinctly described as "a five-million dollar celebration of Gary Cooper's virility, Paulette Goddard's femininity, and the American frontier spirit."

At MGM, producer Arthur Freed initiated an extraordinary series of classic film musicals for the studio, including *Meet Me in St Louis* (1944), *The Pirate* (1948) and *On the Town* (1949). Performers like Judy Garland and Gene Kelly and directors like Vincente Minnelli, Stanley Donen, George Sidney and Charles Walters were to do some of the best work of their life during this period. During the decade there were also a number of highly successful musicals based on the work of Irving Berlin. *Easter Parade* (1948) and *Annie Get Your Gun* (1950) are the most fondly remembered, though, in box-office terms, the biggest success was Warners' *This Is the Army* (1943), in which army recruits put on a revue. George Murphy, Joan Leslie and Ronald Reagan were amongst the personnel involved in this mammoth musical morale-booster in Technicolor.

Above: *In **All the King's Men** (1949), a corrupt politician (Broderick Crawford) with mistress, ex-mistress and assassin.*

Authentic black-and-white

Yet the forties was also a great era for the black-and-white drama. Monochrome photography still connoted realism and seriousness of purpose: in fact, all the Best Film Oscars of the decade went to black-and-white movies. It seemed the only possible style for Orson Welles' magnificent study of a newspaper magnate, *Citizen Kane* (1941) – it is, after all, the color of newsprint – and it brought a documentary authenticity to films like Billy Wilder's study of alcoholism, *The Lost Weekend* (1945), Elia Kazan's indictment of anti-Semitism, *Gentleman's Agreement* (1947), and Robert Rossen's exposure of political corruption, *All the King's Men* (1949). Each of these films was voted best of its year by the Hollywood Academy, and each represented a new honesty of approach in its attitude to controversial subject-matter.

More films now began to be shot on location, an acknowledgement that audiences were becoming more sophisticated and also a response to the new demand for authenticity. More films were now breaking free from studio constraints, and there was room for smaller, more personal projects. An independent producer like Stanley Kramer came up with hard-hitting films like *Home of the Brave* and *Champion* (1949).

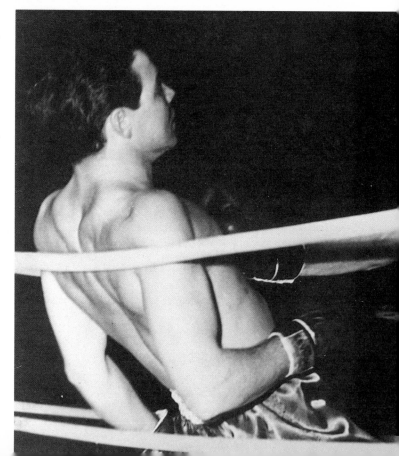

Writers like Billy Wilder, John Huston, Preston Sturges and Joseph L. Mankiewicz began directing their own scripts, mainly because it was the best means of ensuring that the movie maintained the integrity of the basic material. Sturges made a string of great comedies – including *The Great McGinty* (1940), *Sullivan's Travels* (1941) and *Hail the Conquering Hero* (1944) – that satirized American sacred cows. Wilder demonstrated his versatility by supplementing the dramatic *Lost Weekend* with a classic thriller, *Double Indemnity* (1944), and the best film ever made about Hollywood, *Sunset Boulevard* (1950). Huston began a fruitful association with Humphrey Bogart that included the doyen of private-eye movies, *The Maltese Falcon* (1941), and a classic allegory of greed, *The Treasure of the Sierra Madre* (1948). Mankiewicz won Oscars in consecutive years for writing and directing *A Letter to Three Wives* (1949) and *All About Eve* (1950), two impeccably stylish comedies of manners and morality.

Bottom: *Kirk Douglas is a **Champion** (1949) on his way to the top by any means – but finally marked for death.*

Above: *Dorothy McGuire, Gregory Peck and Sam Jaffe in **Gentleman's Agreement** (1947).* **Below:** *Ray Milland as an alcoholic who hallucinates when DTs strike in **The Lost Weekend** (1945).*

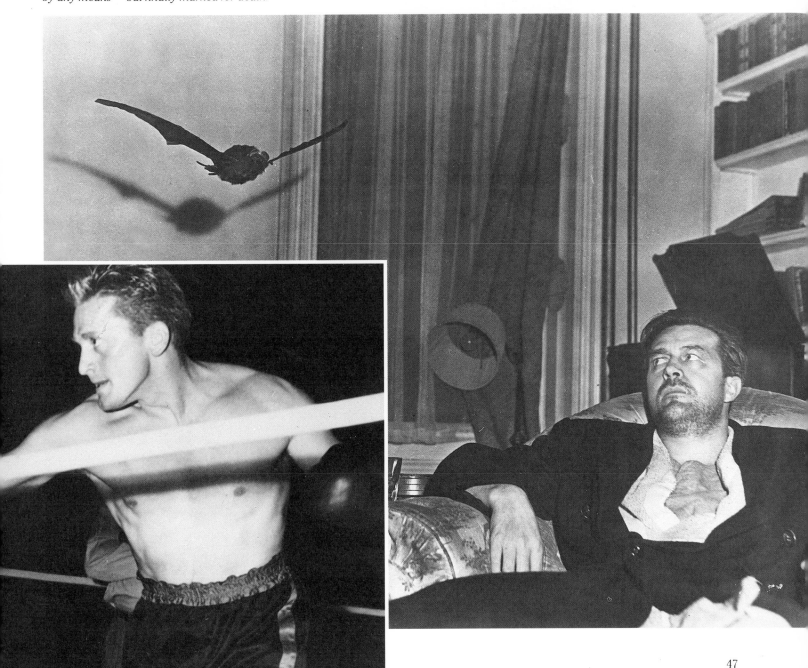

47

Top: *A crooked politician (Brian Donlevy) is influenced by a good woman (Muriel Angelus) in **The Great McGinty** (1940).*
Above: *A film director (Joel McCrea) sets out to discover real life in **Sullivan's Travels** (1941).*
Right: *Insincere congratulations from Bette Davis and Gary Merrill to Anne Baxter (as Eve) on winning a theatrical award while critic George Sanders looks on in **All About Eve** (1950).*

The War inevitably had an impact on the sensibilities of both audiences and film makers – particularly on those directors who had been engaged on active service. William Wyler made the great American film about the aftermath of war, *The Best Years of Our Lives* (1946); Frank Capra made his most intense, troubled and poetic hymn to the indomitability of man, *It's a Wonderful Life* (1946); George Stevens, who had been a member of the American forces that liberated Dachau, was, so to speak, shellshocked into silence until *I Remember Mama* in 1948 – "a story of the confirmed period of the past," as Stevens put it, "dissociated from all the unresolved present." The gangster movie resumed, but the world had seen too much of the effects of megalomania and ruthless ambition to resume the thirties portrait of the gangster as romantic outsider or tragic hero. Now he was portrayed as a bully and a psychopath. Edward G. Robinson's Johnny Rocco in Huston's *Key Largo* (1948) is a menacing figure symbolic of the threat that can be posed to American democratic institutions if evil is not opposed. James Cagney's demonic Cody Jarrett in Raoul Walsh's excellent *White Heat* (1949) is a character whose individualism has been wrenched and twisted into murderous mania.

Down dark streets

The atmosphere of foreboding was especially prominent in a series of black-and-white thrillers – later to be categorized as *film noir* – which were among the richest and most interesting Hollywood products of the period. These were films about tough guys and brazen broads, and they reflected a world that was not only morally more complex than before but also infinitely more brutal. They included labyrinthine detective stories like Otto Preminger's *Laura* (1944) and Howard Hawks' *The Big Sleep* (1946), in which an investigator is compelled to explore a world of ambiguous sexuality and terrifying moral corruption.

Above: *James Stewart gallantly offers to help scantily clad Donna Reed in* **It's a Wonderful Life** *(1946).*

Below: *Waiting for Rocco at a hotel in* **Key Largo** *(1948) are a veteran (Humphrey Bogart), the proprietress (Lauren Bacall) and Rocco's gang (Marc Lawrence, Thomas Gomez, Dan Seymour).*

Many of the most noted of these films were directed by European emigrés – Wilder's *Double Indemnity* (1944), Lang's *Scarlet Street* (1945), Siodmak's *The Killers* (1946) – who infused their plots with a brooding visual style and an angst-ridden atmosphere that seemed to derive from European terrors of the previous years of which they had personal knowledge. The heroes were doomed and fatalistic; the heroines were alarming, independent sexual sirens who could not be trusted; and the action took place in an atmosphere of urban oppression where, in Raymond Chandler's memorable phrase, "the streets were dark with something more than night."

However, this courageous Hollywood attempt to treat more serious themes in an endeavor to appeal to more discriminating audiences was cut short. During the Cold War period of the late forties and early fifties, the House UnAmerican Activities Committee (HUAC) began an investigation into Communist infiltration of Hollywood. A grim period of blackballing, blacklisting and betrayal followed, and movies that were pessimistic and/or honestly critical about aspects of American society ran the risk of being branded as dangerously subversive. After the euphoria of the box-office boom in 1946, Hollywood suddenly found itself under siege from three quite different forces: HUAC, the rise of television, and the decline of audiences. The forties drew to a close on a distinctly downbeat note.

Below: *Following a prison break, Cody (James Cagney) surprises his double-dealing wife (Virginia Mayo) about to desert her lover in **White Heat** (1949).*

Above: *An insurance investigator (Edward G. Robinson, right) and a salesman involved in a murder plot (Fred MacMurray) are unlikely friends in* **Double Indemnity** *(1944).*

Favorites of the forties: swimming star Esther Williams **(above)**, *Gary Cooper (in the 1952 classic* **High Noon**) **(right)**, *comics Abbott* and *Costello* **(top right)**, *palefaces Jane Russell and Bob Hope* **(top, far right)**.

The biggest hits
The ten most popular movies of the decade were, in order: *The Best Years of Our Lives* (1946); *Duel in the Sun* (1947); *This is the Army* (1943); *The Jolson Story* (1946); *Going My Way* (1944); *The Bells of St Mary's* (1945); *Sergeant York* (1941); *For Whom the Bell Tolls* (1943); *Mrs Miniver* (1942); *Spellbound* (1945).

The biggest stars
The most popular stars of 1941 to 1945 were, in order: Bob Hope, Gary Cooper, Abbott and Costello, Bette Davis, Bing Crosby, Greer Garson, Clark Gable, Mickey Rooney, Humphrey Bogart, Spencer Tracy. And between 1946 and 1950 the Top Ten stars were: Bing Crosby, Bob Hope, Betty Grable, Gary Cooper, Abbott and Costello, Humphrey Bogart, Ingrid Bergman, John Wayne, Cary Grant, Esther Williams.

Adventure
SERGEANT YORK (WB 1941)
Director: Howard Hawks

Alvin C. York was the most famous American hero of World War I, decorated for his bravery in shooting 20 enemy soldiers singlehanded. In dealing with a period of the war when America had finally joined the conflict, Hawks' film was implicitly asking audiences to draw a parallel with the present situation: it is covertly an exhortation for America to join World War II. However, unlike the direct appeal that concludes two films by English emigrés, Chaplin's *The Great Dictator* (1940) and Hitchcock's *Foreign Correspondent* (1940), *Sergeant York* expresses its theme and its intentions more obliquely. For its first audiences, it could be taken on its surface level as a rousing celebration of a great American hero. The force and appeal of its polemical undercurrent only became apparent later.

The good fight
It was widely thought within the industry that audiences did not at this time want war movies, and *Sergeant York* skilfully conceals that it is one for a long time. The early scenes recreate York's background as a Tennessee mountaineer, struggling to secure a living from the soil so he can prove himself worthy of marrying his sweetheart. The determination and idealism that he shows are later to be elaborated in his bravery on the battlefield, when this quiet American overcomes his religious doubts and is roused to action against evil.

Gary Cooper is ideally cast as York. "You'd watch him do a scene," said Hawks about directing Cooper, "and you'd go home worrying about whether you had it. And then you'd look next day at the rushes – and there was more there than you wanted in the first place." The performance was to win Cooper an Oscar. He is finely supported by the splendid Margaret Wycherly as his mother (she was to play James Cagney's much more alarming mother in the 1949 classic, *White Heat*), and Hawks directs with characteristic fluency, being rewarded with, surprisingly, his one and only Oscar nomination for direction.

Typically for Hawks, the tone alternates between gritty realism, notably in the scenes on the battlefield, and folksy humor, particularly in the early Tennessee scenes and even in those in which York commits his killings. John Huston co-wrote the screenplay, and the material has certain ironies that seem in retrospect more characteristic of Huston than of Hawks – the situation of a man who kills in order to stop the killing, and of a man who is subsequently honored and remembered for acts which go against the religious beliefs that have formed his character.

Call to arms
Mainly Hawks plays it for the adventure. By choosing the First rather than the Second World War as his focus, Hawks can advocate action without seeming explicitly to drag Hollywood into the current European conflict. At the same time, by having an *American* rather than European hero at the center, he can make the issues of freedom for which York was fighting and over which Europe is now struggling that much more relevant to an American audience.

54

Sergeant York was released in September 1941, only three months before the events around Pearl Harbor were to vindicate the film's implicit questioning of America's isolationist stance. It remains basically the story of an individual's struggle with his conscience and beliefs, a story that pays more attention to entertainment values than to making political points.

Nevertheless the film's great commitment to principled action at a period of global turmoil proved to be timely, important and overwhelmingly popular. It anticipated the mood of a nation, and, in box-office terms, reaped the benefits of that mood.

Left: *An ambitious studio set for* **Sergeant York** *(1941) with director Howard Hawks seated near camera and Gary Cooper on the rock. This shot illustrates the prewar Hollywood preference for bringing the world into the studio.*

Below: *Private York (Cooper) and his mates, including Pusher Rose (George Tobias – left), contemplating the death of a friend. Pusher will be the next one on the hit list.*

War
MRS MINIVER (MGM 1942)
Director: William Wyler

Although it won six Hollywood Oscars, *Mrs Miniver* is less well remembered today for its artistic merit than for its propagandist force. Begun on 11 November 1941, *Mrs Miniver* was Wyler's attempt to advocate direct involvement in the war. The head of MGM, Louis B. Mayer, was rather uneasy during the early stages of production, particularly with the characterization of the downed German flyer, whom Mrs Miniver is compelled to shoot. America had not yet joined the war, and the ultra-conservative Mayer did not want MGM to be suspected of attempting to influence political policy. Wyler was insistent that the only German character to appear in the film had to symbolize what the war was about and that therefore the character, in Wyler's words, had "got to be one of Goering's little monsters." After Pearl Harbor, Mayer withdrew his objections.

Bringing the message home
Why did *Mrs Miniver* have such an impact, when other distinguished, thematically similar films of the time – Hitchcock's *Foreign Correspondent* (1940), Borzage's *The Mortal Storm* (1940), Lang's *Man Hunt* (1941), Litvak's *This Above All* (1942) – did not? The main reason is that *Mrs Miniver* concentrated not on the external reality of the war, but on the meaning of it to an average yet idealized family. The film includes the reality of air-raids and deals with the evacuation of Dunkirk, but the focus is exclusively on how such events affect the Minivers. They come to stand not simply for England but for the whole notion of family life. An audience might not easily identify with a country but it could do so with the situation of a particular family under threat, which gives a forceful human dimension to their opposition to the Nazi menace.

Wyler emphasizes this theme by his careful establishing of the domestic routine. A long opening sequence establishes the ease and intimacy of the marriage: Mrs Miniver has secretly bought a hat, Mr Miniver has secretly bought a car, and both are amusingly wary of telling the other of their extravagance. The growing tragedy of the war is dramatized in an unconventional way. Mrs Miniver has to kill a German flyer in her own home, an improbable event realistically, but symbolically crucial to Wyler's theme: the necessity of involving *everyone* in the struggle to defend home and country. Mrs Miniver's son is taken off to war, and one anticipates the worst. Unexpectedly, however, it is the daughter-in-law who is to be killed in an air-raid. In the final church service scene, the chaplain puts into words why they must fight:

"This is not only a war of soldiers in uniform, it is a war of the people – of all the people – and it must be fought, not only on the battlefield, but in the cities and in the villages, in the factories and on the farms, in the home and in the heart of every man, woman and child who love freedom. Well, we have buried our dead, but we shall not forget them. Instead, they will inspire us with an unbreakable determination to free ourselves and those who come after us from the tyranny and terror that threaten to strike us down. Fight it, then! Fight it with all that is in us! And may God defend the right!"

A woman's role
Of course, the film's evocation of England is unreal and fantasized – all flower shows and tea parties, with Dame May Whitty and Henry Travers representing the upper and lower classes respectively. Although Wyler makes a few characteristic points about the tensions of class and privilege, the main concern is to bolster British morale and sell the war to the American public. He does it by extolling the sanctity of family life and through Greer Garson's strong playing of Mrs Miniver.

Ironically, Miss Garson originally had misgivings over the role, fearing Wyler's tyrannical reputation, and feeling she was too young to be playing the mother of a twenty-year-old son (by an odd coincidence, she was to marry the man who played her son in the film, Richard Ney). But it is her most memorable screen performance and won her an Oscar. Through her, the film presents a refreshing feminine perspective on the war, refusing to treat women as mere spectators in the struggle and showing what strong women could do.

Wyler was shortly to join the Air Force and make war documentaries before returning to Hollywood to reflect on the aftermath of war in *The Best Years of Our Lives* (1946). When he finally saw *Mrs Miniver*, even the normally tough Wyler was moved by it. "Christ, what a tear-jerker," he said. Audiences at the time, and since, have continued to reach for the Kleenex.

Right: *The unlikely Mrs Miniver turns killer, but it's in a good cause as she defends home and country against the Nazis.*

Below: *Mrs Miniver (Greer Garson) and her husband (Walter Pidgeon) facing up to the dangers of war as their son goes off to fight – although it is their daughter-in-law who is eventually killed.*

Romance
RANDOM HARVEST (MGM 1942)
Director: Mervyn LeRoy

"I would like to recommend *Random Harvest*," said the critic James Agee in 1942, "to those who can stay interested in Ronald Colman's amnesia for two hours, and who could with pleasure eat a bowl of Yardley's shaving soap for breakfast." There were many more such people than Agee clearly suspected. *Random Harvest* was the most popular romantic film of the decade, more so than famous films like *Casablanca* (1943) and *Since You Went Away* (1944).

A plot summary by the film historian Leslie Halliwell gives an appropriate impression of the material's romantic licence: "A shell-shocked officer in the 1914-18 war escapes from an asylum, marries a music-hall singer and is idyllically happy until a shock makes him remember that he is the head of a noble family. His wife, whom he does not now remember, dutifully becomes his secretary and years later another shock brings memory and happiness back." The cast plays it for all it is worth, and more, and contemporary audiences went for that kind of entertainment in a big way, secure in the knowledge that these prisoners of past obsessions will eventually come to terms with the situation and that a happy ending is guaranteed.

Random Harvest is what is often disparagingly referred to as a "woman's picture" – that is, it is emotional, glossy, escapist and essentially about feelings. Nevertheless, weepies like this must still touch some truth about human nature for people to respond to them so readily. The plot might seem absurd, but the theme of love and sacrifice must have struck a number of relevant chords for women (and men, thinking about their women) during the war years. From a feminine perspective, *Random Harvest* can be viewed as a project about the martyrdom of marital and material instincts in the female, and the rewards that must eventually come with romantic fidelity and with unselfish renunciation of one's own desires in favor of a dedication to one's husband. As many women are asked – and prepared – to do still, the heroine of *Random Harvest* risks everything for love. Her life and survival are essentially determined by her commitment to the man she has married. She is rewarded when her partner simultaneously recognizes her self-sacrifice and acknowledges her identity.

Romantic sacrifice was a common fate of screen heroines of the 1940s, and various actresses attempted similar roles. There was often a thin line between martyrdom and masochism in the "suffering womanhood" roles of Joan Crawford (notably in the 1945 *Mildred Pierce*) and Jane Wyman (in the 1948 *Johnny Belinda*), whereas Ingrid Bergman brought a nobility to her emotional roles in *For Whom the Bell Tolls* (1943), *Casablanca* and *Gaslight* (1945) and Joan Fontaine's bruised heroines had a touching vulnerability in *Rebecca* (1940), *Suspicion* (1941) and *Letter From an Unknown Woman* (1948).

The most popular actress for this kind of role in the early 1940s, however, was Greer Garson, perhaps because she seemed the least exceptional, the closest to real life. Her passions never seemed to diminish her practicality: whatever the state of her love, there was always a resilience that made her get on with living, and wait for things to work themselves out. She did not have sufficient dramatic range to move us as deeply as the other actresses, but, unlike them on occasions, she never descended to morbidity. She projected an instinct for survival, even during difficult times. In 1942, that was a valuable thing to do.

Below and right: *When amnesiac Smithy (Ronald Colman) plays truant from a military hospital and meets a showgirl (Greer Garson), he falls in love and marries her. But a street accident restores his former identity and he forgets her.*

RANDOM
HARVEST

RONALD
Colman · Garson
GREER

Prisonniers
du Passé

d'après le roman de JAMES HILTON
Mise en Scène MERVYN LE ROY

59

Fantasy/Horror
CAT PEOPLE (RKO 1942)
Director: Jacques Tourneur

"Try to make a film called *Cat People*," said the head of RKO to producer Val Lewton. "It's a good title." On this flimsy premise, Lewton and his writer, DeWitt Bodeen, went to work. They came up with a story of a young woman who is a descendant of a Serbian cat cult and who turns into a ferocious panther when her passions are aroused. With the support of director Jacques Tourneur, the splendid RKO cameraman Nicholas Musuraca and the composer Roy Webb, the team went on to fashion one of the most ingenious and successful of B-thrillers.

The effectiveness of the film is particularly enhanced by the technique. Val Lewton's aim was to convey horror by suggestion, so the film works very powerfully on an audience's imagination without visual distortion and without needing to show anything explicitly gory or horrific. An extraordinary use of sound and shadow makes the scene where a girl is terrorized in the swimming pool a classic of cinematic suspense. Lewton, Tourneur and the editor, Mark Robson developed a sharp editing technique to intensify a scene where a girl is being chased through a park. From a close-up of the girl running down a street in terror, the film cuts to a shot of a bus as it grinds to a halt with a loud hissing of brakes – a sound which, as Robson said, "would knock people out of their seats in a theater."

Left: *Irena Dubrovna (Simone Simon), a Serbian artist, believes she is descended from a race of cat-women who, when sexually aroused, turn into panthers. Although she agrees to marry Oliver Reed (Kent Smith) she refuses to consummate the marriage lest she turns too wild and ends up by killing him.*

Right: *Oliver turns for consolation to Alice (Jane Randolph – center), so angering his wife that she succumbs to her savage instincts and pursues the girl with a mixture of jealous fury and discreetly hinted desire. Subsequently Alice is twice attacked… by a giant cat.*

Psychological horror

Clearly there was enough here to keep *aficionados* of the horror film happy. However, contrary to the evidence of his films' lurid advertising, Val Lewton was an extremely tasteful and talented man whose intelligence attracted another level of audience as well (in addition to the attention and admiration of the critics). His films are a skilful blend of the ordinary and the fantastic. They deal with complex psychology, and are full of erudite literary references. *Cat People* begins with a quotation from Freud and ends with one from John Donne's Holy Sonnets ("But black sin hath betrayed to endless night/My world, both parts, and both parts must die"). The heroine's state of mind might have a supernatural explanation, but it has also a convincing sense of sexual ambiguity and repression, as the arousal of her sexuality drives her into anger against men and passion towards women. She is a divided character, who both inspires fear and frightens herself, and the film develops into a tense and tragic study of a divided character without diminishing the suspense and shocks.

According to Jacques Tourneur, the film had such an impact on audiences because it showed, unconsciously but convincingly, that we all live in fear. We are all, said Tourneur, prey to terrifying apprehensions that we do not wish to analyze. "So when the audience sitting in a darkened room recognizes its own insecurity in that of the characters in the film," he said, "then you can show unbelievable situations in the certain knowledge that the audience will follow you."

A hit for RKO

Tourneur's explanation might seem something of a rationalization after the event. Nevertheless, to the amazement of the RKO bosses, the film was a tremendous success. In the early years of the decade, RKO had been having a hard time. The industry joke was that one should head to RKO in the event of an air-raid "because they haven't had a hit for years". But *Cat People* beat the record for the longest exclusive run at an RKO theater, held by *Citizen Kane*. It precipitated a distinguished series of similarly philosophical horror movies from Lewton and his team, such as *I Walked with a Zombie* (1943) and *The Seventh Victim* (1943). Minnelli's Hollywood drama *The Bad and the Beautiful* (1952) paid an explicit homage to the film, and Hitchcock's *The Birds* (1963) has many conscious similarities to *Cat People* (Hitchcock was an enormous admirer of Lewton). More recently in 1982, Paul Schrader made a gory remake, starring Nastassja Kinski. Lewton's film might have made slightly less money than Universal's remake of *The Phantom of the Opera* (1943) with Claude Rains, but it deserves precedence as the horror film of the decade, because it was more successful in relation to cost and incalculably more influential.

Musical
MEET ME IN ST LOUIS (MGM 1944)
Director: Vincente Minnelli

Based on the *New Yorker* reminiscences of Sally Benson, *Meet Me in St Louis* is an intimate musical, with no really big production numbers. Much of its charm stems from its 1903 period detail and its skill in introducing the music within the context of ordinary life. The success of the film elevated Minnelli into the big league of directors and, for some, it is the first indubitably great MGM musical.

The movie is divided into four seasons, each being introduced by a filigreed illustration of the American Gothic house of the Smith family. Summer serves as an introduction to the main characters. The Fall section includes the news that the father is to be transferred to New York, taking his family with him, just before the World's Fair is due to come to St Louis. The Halloween sequence of the film, where the children dress up as demons, is a powerful expression of their child-like frustrations at the adult world. The mood darkens still further in the winter section, culminating in the destruction by Tootie (Margaret O'Brien) of her beloved snowmen – symbolically an attack on parent figures – which compels the father to change his mind about leaving. Spring sees the opening of the World's Fair.

Family unity
Much of the film's appeal lies in its unusual blend of realism, fairy-tale and horror. There are reminders of *The Wizard of Oz* in the use of color, in the casting of Judy Garland and in the way the film vividly makes one feel the imagination of children and the sometimes nightmarish quality of their world. *Meet Me in St Louis* is a family film in quite a complex sense. Its main theme is the necessity of keeping the family together, a theme of obvious appeal at the time and which has nearly always struck a responsive chord in the hearts of American audiences.

However, as well as being a celebration of family life, it also honestly acknowledges some of the tensions within an ordinary family, notably the difficulty of reconciling the wishes of the father (the family's nominal head) with those of the children (who, with the mother, are seen as its heart). It is a female-dominated film but, interestingly, Minnelli is to return to this theme from the father's point of view in his enormously popular, and excruciatingly painful, comedy, *Father of the Bride* (1950).

Meet Me in St Louis was probably such a success because it appealed to a wide range of tastes. Judy Garland fans could relish her performance of some of her most celebrated songs – the title song, "The Boy Next Door", "Have Yourself a Merry Little Christmas", "The Trolley Song". The children could identify with the frightening intensity of Margaret O'Brien's performance, and the adults with the dignity and warmth of Mary Astor as the mother. The color is striking, the mood attractively nostalgic, and the work a deft combination of the familiar (the wholesome attitude to American home life) and the original (the looseness of the narrative structure and the unusual tension that erupts into various parts of the film). Reality and nightmare, homeliness and horror, jostle intriguingly together in an example of popular cinema at its most stylish and intelligent.

Meet Me in St Louis featuring Judy Garland **(right)** *may seem like "happy families" on the big screen, but a complex network of tensions lurks below the surface.*

GOING MY WAY (Paramount 1944)
Director: Leo McCarey

A modestly budgeted black-and-white picture, *Going My Way* proved to have the perfect box-office mix: a comedy blended with a few serious themes, and a generally uplifting story about slum kids with enough songs thrown in to keep the Bing Crosby fans happy. It won seven Oscars, including two for Leo McCarey (for direction and story) and one for Best Film and Best Song ("Swingin' on a Star"); Bing Crosby (Best Actor) and Barry Fitzgerald (Best Supporting Actor) were both honored for their performances.

The central dramatic interest concerns the conflict between the old-fashioned parish priest, Father Fitzgibbon (Fitzgerald), and a new progressive curate, Father O'Malley (Crosby). The conflict eventually turns to mutual respect when the curate organizes Fitzgibbon's reunion with his mother whom he has not seen for thirty years. The sentiment seems deeply felt and is well controlled. Barry Fitzgerald's performance is a rich character study built up, apparently, from the actor's remembrance of a priest in Ireland. The film's affectionate but unblinkered observation of Father Fitzgibbon's cranky irascibility and stubbornness is a reminder that McCarey earlier directed one of the cinema's great films about old age, *Make Way for Tomorrow* (1937). He had also directed some of the previous decade's sharpest comedies, notably *Duck Soup* (1933) and *The Awful Truth* (1937), for which he had won an Oscar, so this film always has a light touch.

Bing's best to date

As a fascinating foil to Fitzgerald, Crosby contributes a performance that seems spry and spontaneous. He had been a top recording and film star for a decade prior to this, but *Going My Way* was unquestionably his finest film opportunity to that date. (Later he was to show a gift for more serious, dramatic roles, notably as the alcoholic singer in the 1954 drama, *The Country Girl*.) His relaxed performance gives a completely unsanctimonious feeling to Father O'Malley, which not only prevents the film from being too sentimental but makes his impact on the young people in the community more convincing.

There is no doubt that the film arrived at just the right time. It came in the middle of a popular vogue for religious films like *The Song of Bernadette* (1943) and *The Keys of the Kingdom* (1944). It also seemed to tie in with a preference for a warmer style of comedy, after the hard-hitting, socially conscious comedies of previous years. McCarey appeared to stand ideally between the populist sentimentality of Capra, without the social message, and the abrasive mockery of Preston Sturges, without the assault on sacred cows. *Going My Way* is leisurely and not aggressive, and delights in characters rather than denounces them. Unusually, the sequel, *The Bells of St Mary's* (1945), was almost as good and even more popular.

Going My Way combined all the right elements for a mid-1940s success; good songs, warm humor and a lively plot informed by the conflicting lifestyles of Bing Crosby and Barry Fitzgerald as curate and priest of a run-down city parish.

SPELLBOUND (Selznick/UA 1945)
Director: Alfred Hitchcock

"Will he kiss or kill me?" Gregory Peck gives Ingrid Bergman an emotional future while she, in return, exorcizes his inarticulate and murderous nightmares.

Ingrid Bergman once attributed Alfred Hitchcock's success to "his very vivid imagination. The whole thing is so personal. I just don't understand how he can ever miss." Although *Rebecca* (1940) and *Notorious* (1946) were also big box-office draws, *Spellbound* was Hitchcock's most prodigious commercial success of the decade.

A doctor (Gregory Peck) in a psychiatric hospital is suspected as an impostor and possible murderer. He also turns out to be tormented by recurrent inexplicable nightmares involving the color white and parallel lines. Through the agency of a fellow doctor (Ingrid Bergman), who has fallen in love with him, his trauma is explained and thus exorcized. In the process, the real murderer is unmasked.

Both the central relationship and the casting were ideally suited to the tastes of the time. A number of films of the mid-forties (Billy Wilder's 1945 drama, *The Lost Weekend,* is a good example) cast the woman in the role of saviour, though not to the extent of emasculating the hero. Bergman's psychiatrist exudes competence but she is also emotionally unfulfilled. Peck's hero clearly needs help but, outside of his illness, he is dependable and strong. She restores him to mental health, while he saves her from a frigid future. The first kiss between them is followed by one of Hitchcock's most impudent Freudian images: a tracking shot of a series of doors opening one after the other.

The casting enhanced the impact of the romance. At this stage of her career, Ingrid Bergman was one of the great romantic stars of the decade. Peck was just beginning to become a heart-throb. According to producer David O. Selznick, at the preview of *Spellbound,* "we could not keep the audience quiet from the time Peck's name first came on the screen until we had shushed the audience three or four times …"

Mental humor

In addition to the appeal of Bergman and Peck, the film also could exploit its fashionable Freudian themes. Both Selznick and the writer Ben Hecht had been under psychoanalysis themselves at some time in their lives and were clearly fascinated by the subject. Hecht brought a characteristic wit to the project. "Good night and sweet dreams," says the professor (Michael Chekhov) to Peck and Bergman, before adding mischievously, "which we will analyze at breakfast."

There is also the daunting combination of Alfred Hitchcock and the outrageous surrealist, Salvador Dali. Hitchcock brought in Dali to do the dream sequences not as a publicity stunt, he insisted, but because he wanted to have the dream photographed very vividly. According to Ingrid Bergman, the original dream sequence lasted nearly twenty minutes and was an "art movie" in its own right. Nowadays, this sequence, which was considerably abbreviated from the original idea, looks rather literal and simplistic (a "wheel" in the dream comes to mean "revolver" for example). At the time, its striking visual presentation and its intriguing imagistic suggestions of the way childhood trauma can lead to neurotic adult behavior seemed unusual and compelling.

Private fantasies

In fact, everyone is more or less mad in *Spellbound* – a "momma's boy" policeman, an obsessive hotel detective, an eccentric railway porter. Although the film is ultimately intended as, in Hitchcock's words, a "sensible study of psychoanalysis", one feels that in his deepest heart Hitchcock believes that people have private and violent fantasies that are only precariously kept under control. Hitchcock gave vent to his own fantasies in his films, contriving intense romantic relationships, blatant sexual imagery, and extraordinarily heightened moments of suspense. A good example of Hitchcock's bizarre visual imagination and his suspense tactics occurs in the denouement of *Spellbound,* as the real killer is revealed. A giant hand points a gun at Bergman as she leaves the room, then turns it to the camera and fires, and a sudden red flash suffuses the screen.

The themes of *Spellbound* were to be treated in greater depth in Hitchcock's later film *Marnie* (1964), where red flashes are not simply a momentary frisson for the audience but a crucial symptom of her trauma. *Spellbound* has not much depth but a great deal of panache. Its commercial performance was undoubtedly enhanced by its somewhat lurid advertising (an apprehensive Bergman being embraced by Peck with an open razor in his hand, and the caption, "Will he kiss me or kill me?"), and by a rhapsodic main theme from Miklos Rozsa that became enormously popular. Indeed, the film boosted the appeal of Freud to such an extent that unscrupulous psychiatrists began advertising their services by falsely claiming to have been involved in the production of *Spellbound.* Such was the power and influence of film in 1945. Though not now regarded as one of Hitchcock's best, it still casts quite a spell.

THE JOLSON STORY (Columbia 1946)

Director: Alfred E. Green

The idea for a film biography of the singer Al Jolson, using Jolson's own singing voice over the soundtrack, originated with columnist-turned-producer Sidney Skolsky. It was enthusiastically supported by Columbia studio chief, Harry Cohn, who idolized Jolson. He was also sensitive to the fact that musical biographies were very popular, particularly after the success of *Yankee Doodle Dandy* (1942) with James Cagney in his Oscar-winning role as George M. Cohan.

True to the formula, the biography would be a sentimentalized version of the truth, with a sketchy sense of period, a respectful and discreet investigation of the star's love life, and the usual alternations of triumph and tragedy that are heightened by the star's fame and by his being constantly in the public eye. The question was: would the public be interested in Jolson, who was 58 by the time of the movie and no longer that popular?

Rivalry of fame

The film partially solved this problem by hitting on a compelling dramatic structure. According to the writer Sidney Buchman: "The story is a love affair. The lover is applause. Jolson's wife could handle another woman, but she was no match for the applause." The film therefore balances the sadness of the break-up of Jolson's marriage to Ruby Keeler (in the film called "Julie Benson", at Miss Keeler's insistence) with the triumph of Jolson as a stage performer. Part of the appeal of the biopic has always been the conflict and contrast between the subject's public and private life.

By stressing Jolson as a pioneer who goes his own way, creates his own style and breaks through popular prejudices, the film cleverly emphasizes Jolson's career as an essentially *American* success story, a triumph of self-confidence and individualism. The songs are chosen carefully to show Jolson to his best advantage – "Rockabye Your Baby With a Dixie Melody", "My Mammy", "You Made Me Love You", "Toot Toot Tootsie", "California Here I Come", and "April Showers".

Mixed appeal

The film succeeded in attracting two kinds of audience. The first was the audience who remembered the phenomenal popularity of Jolson in the twenties, when he made his famous appearance in the first talkie, *The Jazz Singer*, and when even *The New York Times* was praising him for turning "the base metals of vulgarity and sentimentality into pure gold". The second was a younger audience whose taste in popular song was probably for Crosby or Sinatra but who could appreciate Jolson's acknowledged influence on their favorites. The film could be enjoyed too for its dramatic verve. As Jolson, Larry Parks scored a personal triumph in his first major role, and along with the infallible William Demarest as his crusty side-kick and manager, he was nominated for an Oscar.

When the inevitable sequel came, *Jolson Sings Again* (1949), this too was tremendously popular. It resumed Jolson's story up to the success of the film of *The Jolson Story* and it contained one remarkable moment when Parks playing Jolson meets Parks playing Parks, as the actor who, in impersonating Jolson, had revived his career!

Top: Al Jolson (Larry Parks) was primarily known as a stage artist in such shows as **Sonny Boy** (subsequently filmed with only a cameo appearance by him). Later he became a movie star with his blackface tribute to the Jewish momma in the first talkie, **The Jazz Singer.** The film's strength is in its dramatized conflict between Jolson's showbiz success and his unsatisfactory private life. His screen wife was played by Evelyn Keyes **(left).**

THE BEST YEARS OF OUR LIVES
(Goldwyn/RKO 1946)
Director: William Wyler

Producer Samuel Goldwyn and director William Wyler had made several successful films together, including *Dodsworth* (1936), *Dead End* (1937), *Wuthering Heights* (1939) and *The Little Foxes* (1941). But their biggest hit by far was their final collaboration, *The Best Years of Our Lives*. It represented the high-point of Goldwyn drama, with plush production values, believable characters and an air of social optimism that had proved such a winning formula in the past. The extra ingredient this time was the intense identification with the subject felt by writer Robert E. Sherwood and director William Wyler. Sherwood had written speeches during the war for Roosevelt and Wyler had filmed documentaries in the combat zone, in the process sustaining an injury which was to affect his hearing for the rest of his life. They wanted to do a film about the fate of returning veterans, a film which would analyze the new society for which they had fought and investigate whether their sacrifice had been worthwhile.

The film concentrates on the social re-adjustment of three servicemen, each from a different stratum of society. Al (Fredric March) returns to an influential banking position, but finds it hard to reconcile his loyalties to ex-servicemen with new commercial realities. Fred (Dana Andrews) is an ordinary working man who finds it difficult to hold down a job or pick up the threads of his marriage. Having had both hands burnt off during the war, Homer (real-life amputee Harold Russell) is unsure that his fiancée's feelings are still those of love and not those of pity.

An illusion of reality
The three stories occasionally and ingeniously intersect, with particular tension when Fred starts an affair with Al's daughter Peggy (Teresa Wright) and Al warns him off. Generally speaking, though, the film seems relatively plotless and unobtrusively, compellingly real. Although a number of distinguished films at the time were dealing with the psychological problems of GIs returning from the war, notably *The Blue Dahlia* (1946) and *Crossfire* (1947), these tended to treat the problems through the mode of melo-drama or *film noir*. It is possible that *Best Years* had such a strong appeal, especially in Europe (in England it outgrossed *Gone with the Wind* and it was even popular in Germany), because of its absence of melodrama and its skilful illusion that it was dealing with life-like people with "authentic" problems. For all its ultimate optimism, it is a restrained, subdued, rather melancholy movie, which does not gloss over a new spirit of rampant commercialism nor senti-mentalize the difficulty of re-adjustment. The new post-war film audience was no doubt ready for a film that told it as it was, not as we wished it to be.

A seriousness of purpose
Within the realist structure, the film has some especially sensitive moments of drama: Al's reunion with his wife, filmed in discreet long-shot; Fred's exorcizing of war-time ghosts on a deserted airfield; the ritual of Homer's having to be put to bed. The wedding of Homer and Wilma is brilliantly filmed, so that one is aware that a comment is being made

also on Al's present marriage, Fred's former marriage and the uncertainty of his future with Peggy. It is a long film, but absolutely absorbing, and peerlessly performed and pro-duced. As well as any other Hollywood film, its intelligence, gentle humanity and profound decency seemed to reflect a contemplative and concerned mood in the country at that time. *The Best Years of Our Lives* won the Oscar as Best Picture of the year, as well as Wyler's second directing Oscar, performance Oscars for Russell and March, a writing Oscar for Robert E. Sherwood, and further Oscars for Best Score (Hugo Friedhofer) and Best Editing (Daniel Mandell).

Above: *Ex-Major Fred Derry (Dana Andrews), after brief glory as a flyer, is hit by the mundane postwar world of the local drugstore.*

Left: *Real life amputee Harold Russell (second right) and Fredric March watch Hoagy Carmichael hit the keyboard.*

Western

DUEL IN THE SUN (Selznick 1946)
Director: King Vidor

"Deep among the lonely sunbaked hills of Texas, the great and weatherbeaten stone still stands. The Comanches call it Squaw's Head Rock. Time cannot change its impassive face, nor dim the legend of Pearl, who was herself a wild flower, sprung from the hard clay, quick to blossom and early to die."

Narrated by Orson Welles, these are the opening words of *Duel in the Sun*, the most popular western ever made and a sort of *Wuthering Heights* of the range. It is a "horse opera" in which, for once, the term "opera" is justified, for the film has the courage of its exaggerations and a mad passion that carries all before it. The subject is a traditional western one of the conflict between the farmer and the cowman, and the coming of the railroad. However, the film's main force comes from the love-hate relationship at its center between a satanic cowboy, Lewt (Gregory Peck), and an Indian half-breed, Pearl (Jennifer Jones).

Duel in the Sun was the brainchild of David O. Selznick who, as he had done with *Gone with the Wind*, set out to prove that nothing succeeds like excess. The story is based on a small book by Niven Busch, who also wrote Raoul Walsh's *Pursued* (1947), another passionate story of tangled emotions and family curses. In Selznick's hands, this small tale grew bigger and bigger. Again like *Gone with the Wind*, the director credit conceals more than it reveals. The credited director, King Vidor, who had earlier told Selznick that "I'll compromise on anything if you let me have my own way", walked out two days before the scheduled end of shooting. Other parts of the film were handled by the assistant director, Josef von Sternberg, and the second unit director, Otto Brower, amongst others. The spectacular opening bar-room scene was directed by Selznick regular William Dieterle, who was ultimately responsible for a good quarter of the film.

Below: *An operatic* Liebestod *(love-death) for Pearl Chavez (Jennifer Jones) and Lewt McCanles (Gregory Peck), who destroy each other. Replete with colorful western imagery* **(right)**, *the film centers on Jennifer Jones* **(top right)**, *a demure, dainty lady whom Selznick saw as a sensual love-goddess.*

Intoxicating extremes

The film is all grand gestures and intense emotions, highlighted by an expressive and stylized use of strange, lurid color. Selznick was never one for subtle shades of character. He wanted Pearl to be the ultimate tempestuous tomboy, a half-breed Scarlett O'Hara, and he wanted to make Lewt, as he put it, "the worst son of a bitch that's ever been seen on a motion picture screen". These extremes of characterization undoubtedly expanded the frontiers of the western, whose relatively conventional morality was not to receive such a shaking until Sam Peckinpah, and certainly appealed to audiences who relished the unbridled relationships.

When it was released, *Duel in the Sun* was rather scornfully reviewed, and disdainfully subtitled "Lust in the Dust". Perversely, this might well have attracted the masses all the more to the cinema. Like Howard Hughes' 1943 film, *The Outlaw* (in which a voluptuous Jane Russell warms up a

feverish Billy the Kid), Selznick included the one quality that had been conspicuously absent from westerns before: namely, sex. Also he had created a rare thing – a western with an appeal to women. It is not often that a western is dominated by the feelings of its heroine and by the dynamism of its main female performance, but that is what happens here. The mad and murderous ending, in which the lovers can only find consummation in death, is melodrama at its most awesome and fearless.

Ford was bringing new dimensions of myth, poetry and complex heroism to the western in films like *My Darling Clementine* (1946) and *Fort Apache* (1948), and Howard Hawks was to make the definitive cattle-drive western in *Red River* (1948). But, for the public, the most seductive and intoxicating of forties' westerns was the seething *Duel in the Sun*. Throughout the decade, there was not another film of any genre that was quite like it.

CHAPTER THREE:

THE FIFTIES

When asked in 1959 what were the most encouraging and discouraging film developments of recent years, director Elia Kazan's answer was the same for both questions: "The triumph of television." It was discouraging, Kazan thought, because television was "harmless, acquiescent pap, doping the audience." It was encouraging because, as Kazan said, television "now does the B-pictures and the junk. We have to be good or big to survive – at least we have to try."

Good or big: this was really the option that faced the film industry in the fifties. In terms of quality, the fifties was a fascinating and underrated decade, lacking the nostalgia value of vintage Hollywood but making up for it with a welcome and surprising diversity. The Italian director Vittorio De Sica thought that *A Streetcar Named Desire* (1951) and *On the Waterfront* (1954) represented a genuine breakthrough. "I sat up in my seat when I saw them," he said. "Hollywood was holding a mirror to life and reflecting it in sharp and vivid focus."

Some of Hollywood's greatest directors made some of their greatest films during this decade – John Ford's *The Searchers* (1956), Orson Welles' *Touch of Evil* (1958), Howard Hawks' *Rio Bravo* (1959), Billy Wilder's *Sunset Boulevard* (1950) and *Some Like It Hot* (1959), Alfred Hitchcock's *Rear Window* (1954) and *Vertigo* (1958). New directors like Robert Aldrich and Stanley Kubrick made striking impressions with early films like *Kiss Me Deadly* (1955) and *Paths of Glory* (1957), respectively. Director Anthony Mann made a string of first-rate westerns with James Stewart, including *Bend of the River* (1952) and *The Man from Laramie* (1955). Gene Kelly (with the 1952 *Singin' in the Rain*) and Fred Astaire (with the 1953 *Band Wagon* and the 1956 *Funny Face*) made arguably their greatest musicals; and even Charles Laughton's one and only film as a director, *The Night of the Hunter* (1955), gradually became a cult classic.

Right: *On the Waterfront* (1954) helped set a new Hollywood approach to reality, helped by strong performances from Marlon Brando and Eva Marie Saint.

Far right: A production shot of Marilyn Monroe as band singer Sugar Kane in *Some Like It Hot* (1959). Billy Wilder shot the film in black and white to make the drag appearance of Tony Curtis and Jack Lemmon more convincing, and it also succeeded in making Marilyn Monroe look slightly less overweight.

Some of the new stars made an electric impact: Marlon Brando in *Streetcar*, Montgomery Clift in *A Place in the Sun* (1951), James Dean in *Rebel Without a Cause* (1955). Elizabeth Taylor revealed her qualities as an actress in two Tennessee Williams dramas, *Cat on a Hot Tin Roof* (1958) and *Suddenly Last Summer* (1959). Audrey Hepburn shot to stardom for her masterly performance in William Wyler's romantic comedy, *Roman Holiday* (1953); and demonstrated her versatility with a starkly dramatic characterization in *The Nun's Story* (1959). With *The Seven Year Itch* (1955) and *Bus Stop* (1956), Marilyn Monroe established herself as the most potent screen goddess since Garbo. To survey that list of movies is to remind oneself of an age of quality that has rarely been equalled since.

Bigger, longer and wider than ever

Fifties movies were also big. From the lavish nature of many of the productions, like MGM's *Quo Vadis?* (1952), one might never have realized that the film industry was in serious trouble. On closer inspection, one could spot that the lavishness was symptomatic of the crisis. It was thought that television would be defeated quantitatively if not qualitatively. The threat would be overcome by emphasizing three aspects television could not match at the time: length, color and size of screen.

Two new stars for the fifties. Paul Newman, **left**, *seen here with Elizabeth Taylor in* **Cat on a Hot Tin Roof** *(1958), and James Dean,* **below**, *who became one of the icons of the decade.*

The era of the long film was from 1956 to 1963. Prior to these dates, only two Hollywood blockbusters had run for over three hours at their premiere: *The Great Ziegfeld* (1936) and *Gone with the Wind* (1939). By 1963, the total had gone up to twenty. Color was now becoming more essential for all kind of films, not simply escapist ones. Directors like John Huston, Joseph L. Mankiewicz, George Stevens and William Wyler made their first color feature films in this decade.

Hollywood's main hope at this time, however, was the widescreen. This was the age of complicated special processes: CinemaScope, Cinerama, 3-D, VistaVision, Todd-AO, Camera 65, and the like. Industry veterans like the cameraman Leon Shamroy grumbled: "Oh my God! You got a stage play again, you put pictures back to the earliest sound days, you couldn't even do close-ups because they'd distort so horribly." Yet intelligent directors, like George Cukor with *A Star Is Born* (1954) and Elia Kazan with *East of Eden* (1955), showed that it was possible to use the widescreen expressively. For a short burst between 1954 and 1956, it did look as if the advent of the widescreen had succeeded in halting the downward trend of audiences. *This Is Cinerama* (1952) and *Cinerama Holiday* (1955) were little more than high-class travelogues yet the Cinerama process made them appear exciting and they were very successful. *House of Wax* (1953) was one of the few 3-D successes. It is highly doubtful whether *The Robe* (1953) and *How to Marry a Millionaire* (1953) would have been so successful without CinemaScope, or *White Christmas* (1954) so popular without VistaVision. However, it soon became apparent that color and screen processes alone could not solve the industry's problems.

Left: *Danny Kaye, Vera-Ellen and Bing Crosby in* **White Christmas** *(1954); the film's success was helped along by Irving Berlin's hit song of the same name.*

Below: *In the mid fifties 3-D was used to create box-office hits and win back audiences. The technique yielded a few successes, such as* **House of Wax** *(1953) starring Vincent Price, but Hollywood had to think up other ideas to attract audiences.*

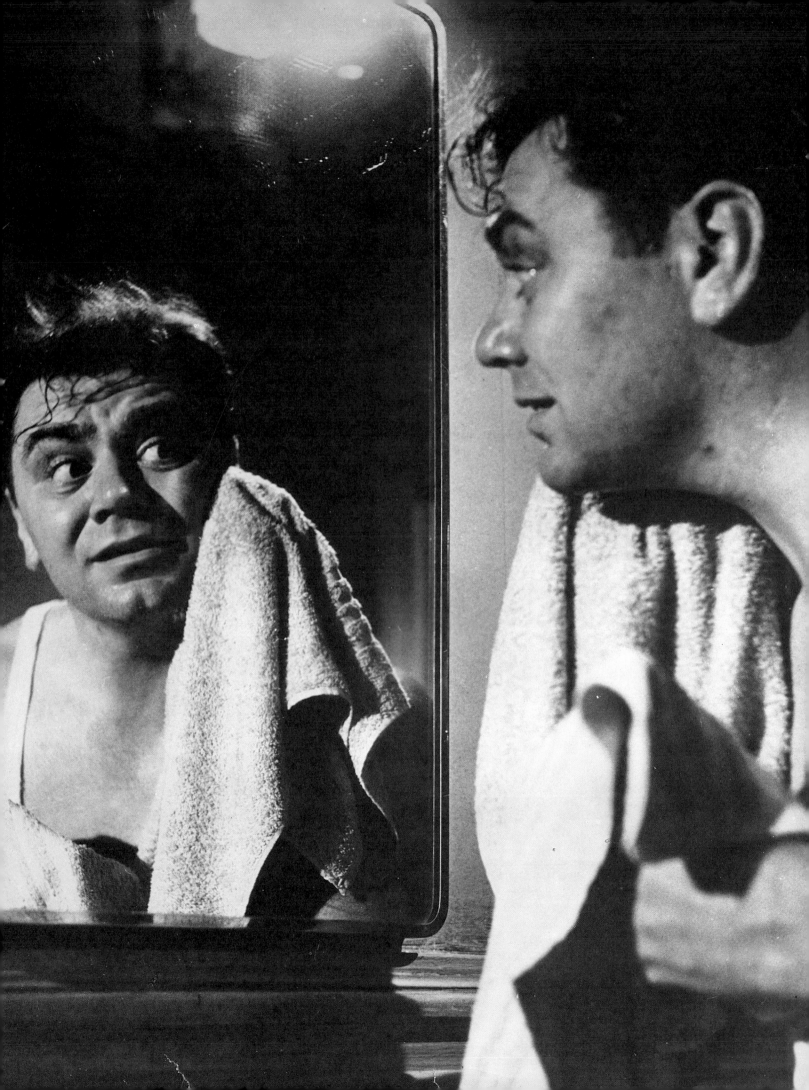

Making use of the enemy

In addition to widening the movie screens, television had an impact and influence in other areas of movie practice. Television provided the movies with a brand new subject to examine and attack, notably in the bitterly satirical musical, *It's Always Fair Weather,* directed by Stanley Donen and Gene Kelly, who three years earlier had been celebrating Hollywood's capacity to adjust to another crisis – the coming of sound – in *Singin' in the Rain.* Quality television drama, however, was often successfully transferred to the screen. Paddy Chayefsky's television play *Marty* became a successful low-budget movie in 1955, winning Oscars for actor Ernest Borgnine and director Delbert Mann. Reginald Rose's *Twelve Angry Men* was another transposition from television in 1957 and highly effective under the direction of Sidney Lumet (his first film).

In general, now that B-movies had been discontinued, American television in the fifties was as good a way as any for the aspiring movie director to learn his craft. Some of the directors who began in television during this decade were to make some of Hollywood's best movies of the following decade – John Frankenheimer's *The Manchurian Candidate* (1962), Robert Mulligan's *To Kill A Mockingbird* (1962), Martin Ritt's *Hud* (1963), Franklin J. Schaffner's *The Best Man* (1964), Arthur Penn's *Bonnie and Clyde* (1967).

Left: *Ernest Borgnine as the Bronx butcher on his way to an Oscar-winning performance in* **Marty** *(1955)*

Below: *Directors of future successes, such as Franklin J. Schaffner with* **The Best Man** *(1964), spent the fifties learning their trade in TV.*

With television at this time aiming almost exclusively at family audiences, the movies were more free to examine material that might have proved too adult or controversial to show on the small screen. Preminger's film about a murder trial involving rape, *Anatomy of a Murder* (1959), would have been an unthinkable subject for a Hollywood movie a few years before, and Preminger made conscientious and responsible use of the industry's more liberal air. So did Billy Wilder with his black comedy about pimping and office politics, *The Apartment* (1960). Both movies were big successes.

In general, the fifties was a rich time for lurid, lucrative and often very powerful melodrama. Vincente Minnelli dealt with psychiatric problems in *The Cobweb* (1955) and sexual hang-ups in *Tea and Sympathy* (1956), whilst Douglas Sirk made a series of delirious melodramas, including *All That Heaven Allows* (1955) and *Imitation of Life* (1959) that comprised a trenchant attack on certain aspects of American puritanism, materialism and intolerance. The steamy dramas of Tennessee Williams were particularly snapped up, though often appearing on the screen in a somewhat modified form. A theater audience might be able to accept the implications of the hero's homosexuality in *Cat on a Hot Tin Roof* (1958), but movie audiences were not yet ready for that. Director Richard Brooks had to find some other convoluted reason for Paul Newman's refusal to bed Liz Taylor, at her most alluring and seductive as Maggie the Cat.

Right: *Imitation of Life (1959), which starred Lana Turner and,* **inset***, Susan Kohner and Sandra Dee.*

Below: *James Stewart as counsel for the defence acting his heart out in **Anatomy of a Murder** (1959).*

End of an era

The major studios all had their fortunes and misfortunes during this turbulent decade. In contrast to the studio-based movies of a previous era when everyone was under contract, the quality of a film now depended most on the individual directors and producers, and there was active competition between the film companies for their services. Independent producers Stanley Kramer and Sam Spiegel switched from United Artists to Columbia during the mid-fifties: their box-office successes such as *The Caine Mutiny* (1954) and *The Bridge on the River Kwai* (1957) considerably enhanced Columbia's status. Similarly, independent producer-director Billy Wilder moved from Paramount to Fox to United Artists, giving big hits to each in turn – respectively, *Stalag 17* (1953), *The Seven Year Itch* and *Some Like It Hot*. With his first two color films, *Shane* (1953) and *Giant* (1956), producer-director George Stevens provided Paramount and Warners respectively with two of the big hits of the decade.

An era came to an end during the fifties. Harry Cohn, who had run Columbia for over thirty years, died in 1958. Darryl Zanuck gave up the post of production chief at Fox in 1956 to embark on a new career as an independent producer. Of the old-time moguls, he alone would return to power in the sixties. David O. Selznick and Sam Goldwyn were reaching the end of their careers in a kind of dignified decline. "I had a monumental idea this morning," Goldwyn would say towards the end of his career, adding, "but I don't like it."

Right: *Shane* (1953) was the biggest personal success for forties and fifties star Alan Ladd.

Below: "Come back, Shane!" The sad cry of Brandon de Wilde in the 1953 film of the same name was answered – not by a Shane II or Shane in 3-D, but by a decade of some of the greatest westerns ever made from top directors including John Ford, Howard Hawks, Robert Aldrich and Arthur Penn.

*The one that made it – **Ben-Hur** (1959) **(top right)** and two that didn't quite, despite the presence of teen idol James Dean in **East of**   **Eden** (1955) **(right)** and Katharine Hepburn in **Suddenly Last Summer** (1959) **(above)**.*

The biggest hits
The Top Ten box-office hits of the fifties, in order, were:
Ben-Hur (1959); The Ten Commandments (1956);
Around the World in 80 Days (1956); The Robe (1953);
South Pacific (1958); The Bridge on the River Kwai
(1957); The Greatest Show on Earth (1952); This Is
Cinerama (1952); From Here to Eternity (1953); Giant
(1956).

The biggest stars
The Top Ten Stars between 1951 and 1955 were, in
order: John Wayne; Dean Martin and Jerry Lewis; Gary
Cooper; James Stewart; Bing Crosby; Bob Hope; Alan
Ladd; Marilyn Monroe; William Holden; Grace Kelly.
And between 1956 and 1960: Rock Hudson; John
Wayne; James Stewart; William Holden; Cary Grant;
Doris Day; Elizabeth Taylor; Glenn Ford; Frank Sinatra;
Jerry Lewis.

Technical experiment
THE ROBE (Fox 1953)
Director: Henry Koster

The fifties was the decade of the widescreen, and the first feature film to exploit it to commercial advantage was *The Robe*, made by 20th Century-Fox in its new widescreen process known as CinemaScope. The process itself had been demonstrated by a Frenchman, Henri Chrétien, as early as 1927, but it was thought to have little or no commercial value. However, in an endeavor to emphasize the superiority of film to television by almost doubling the screen's ratio of width to height (now 2.35:1 rather than the previous 1.33:1), 20th Century-Fox took an option on Chrétien's process, rechristened it, and looked around for an appropriate subject. Predictably, the studio's choice was a biblical one, which permitted spectacle and extras. The critic Pauline Kael cynically remarked: "They appear to be so dazzled by the width of the screen, they feel it can only be filled by God."

Lack of imagination
The invention inevitably had some influence on the technique of the film itself. Apart from a vivid storm and incidental flourishes such as a wide shot of three horses racing excitingly towards the CinemaScope camera, the film is staged rather statically. The editing rhythm is slower than usual, as if to allow an audience time to adjust to the greater space. Director Henry Koster felt CinemaScope made the director less dependent on the cameraman and the film editor, and more dependent on his own staging ability and his sense of composition for a large canvas.

In fact, the film is rather short on imagination, either verbal or visual. It is a very literal piece of work. When a character is introduced washing his hands and saying, "I've had a terrible night", we know we are in the presence of Pontius Pilate (Richard Boone). The title refers to Christ's robe, handed down after the Crucifixion and causing consternation amongst both opponents and followers. Richard Burton plays a Roman who wins the robe in a game of dice; Jean Simmons plays the woman he loves; Victor Mature is one of Christ's followers, Demetrius, a role he was to repeat in the film's sequel, *Demetrius and the Gladiators* (1954). The most colorful performance is provided by Jay Robinson as the insane Caligula who will sentence Burton to death.

Below: *When Victor Mature as the Greek slave refuses to burn the robe saved after the Crucifixion, Richard Burton as the Roman officer tries instead, but fails.*

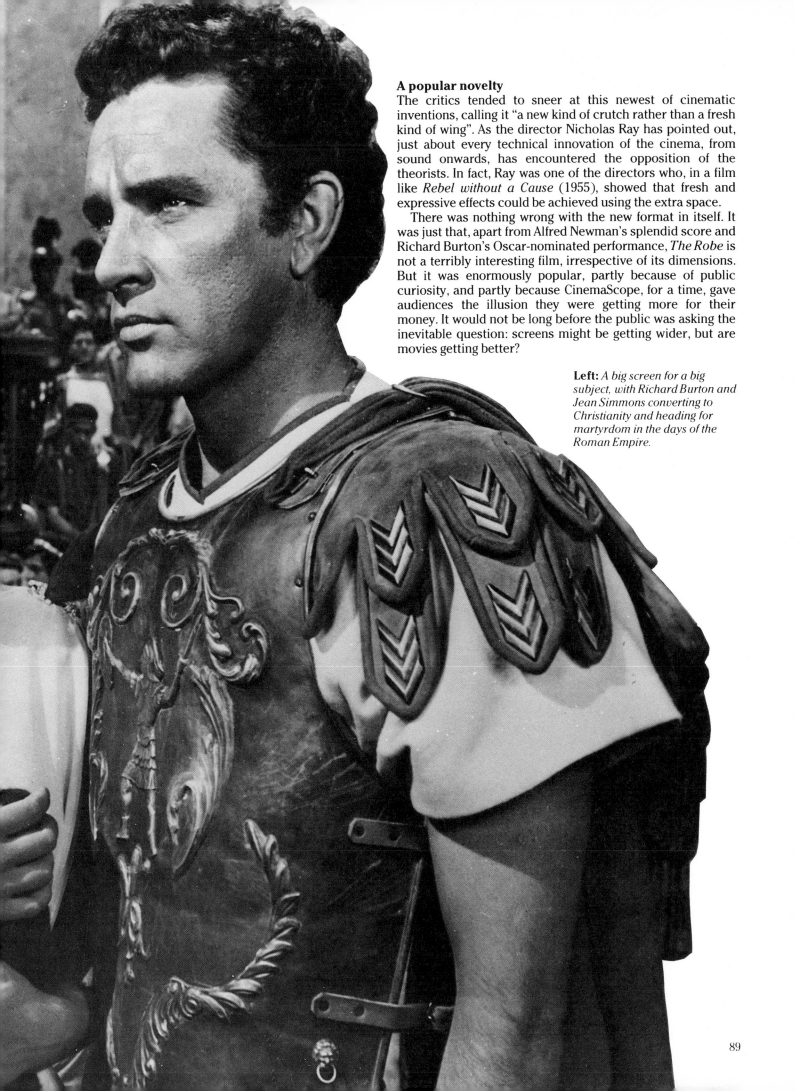

A popular novelty

The critics tended to sneer at this newest of cinematic inventions, calling it "a new kind of crutch rather than a fresh kind of wing". As the director Nicholas Ray has pointed out, just about every technical innovation of the cinema, from sound onwards, has encountered the opposition of the theorists. In fact, Ray was one of the directors who, in a film like *Rebel without a Cause* (1955), showed that fresh and expressive effects could be achieved using the extra space.

There was nothing wrong with the new format in itself. It was just that, apart from Alfred Newman's splendid score and Richard Burton's Oscar-nominated performance, *The Robe* is not a terribly interesting film, irrespective of its dimensions. But it was enormously popular, partly because of public curiosity, and partly because CinemaScope, for a time, gave audiences the illusion they were getting more for their money. It would not be long before the public was asking the inevitable question: screens might be getting wider, but are movies getting better?

Left: *A big screen for a big subject, with Richard Burton and Jean Simmons converting to Christianity and heading for martyrdom in the days of the Roman Empire.*

Drama

FROM HERE TO ETERNITY (Columbia 1953)
Director: Fred Zinnemann

It was known in the industry as "Cohn's Folly". The head of Columbia, Harry Cohn, had acquired the screen rights to James Jones' sizzling bestseller, *From Here to Eternity*. How on earth could the novel's sex, violence and ferociously anti-Army theme be translated into film form (particularly at a time of America's involvement in Korea)? It was achieved essentially through a judicious choice of incident and personnel.

After a number of others had failed, the writer Daniel Taradash came up with a screenplay that seemed to solve the novel's problems for the screen. The sexual content could be suggested rather than shown. The prostitute, Lorene (Donna Reed), would be referred to as a "hostess"; the nymphomania of Karen Holmes (Deborah Kerr) could be implied in a love scene on a beach with Sergeant Warden (Burt Lancaster) in which the surging tide would symbolize passion. Similarly, the violence and the criticism of military life would be implicit rather than explicit. The film would omit showing the brutality of an Army stockade (something the Army insisted on if the film wished to have their co-operation), but it would retain the feeling of harshness by having Maggio (Frank Sinatra) die of his treatment in the stockade rather than simply be badly injured, as he is in the original novel.

Casting against type

The casting of the film was controversial but crucial to its success. Basically, the film worked through casting against type. Burt Lancaster is wary and watchful rather than dynamic as the Sergeant who is having an affair with the Captain's wife. After Eli Wallach had withdrawn from the role of Maggio, Frank Sinatra was cast and reveals an unexpected dramatic range, bringing out his volatility and vulnerability. By giving Donna Reed the role of the "hostess", the film draws attention to the character's bourgeois aspirations more than her sordid situation. The casting of Deborah Kerr as Karen Holmes (after Joan Crawford had made impossible demands about costumes) is so surprising that the audience, as well as the actress, feels challenged: because it is not what moviegoers expect from Miss Kerr, they become that much more curious about the character she is playing.

Above all, the casting of Montgomery Clift as Prewitt, the private who refuses to box for his barracks because he has blinded an opponent in the ring, is essential to the film's effect. Cohn wanted Aldo Ray, partly because Ray looked like a boxer and partly because he was under contract. Director Fred Zinnemann insisted on Clift. "The boxing element didn't interest me at all," said Zinnemann. "I was interested in a man who stuck to his principles no matter what." Clift's portrayal is one of the decade's great anti-hero performances, alongside Brando in *On the Waterfront* (1954) and *The Wild One* (1954) and James Dean in *East of Eden* (1954) and *Rebel without a Cause* (1955). The plight of the individual, who follows his conscience against the dictates and pressures of community, was to be the main theme of all Fred Zinnemann's subsequent major works – *The Nun's Story* (1959), *A Man for All Seasons* (1966) and *Julia* (1977).

Storytelling with skill

Zinnemann had been recommended to Cohn by Daniel Taradash, who had been impressed by his direction of the scenes with the soldiers in *Teresa* (1951). Cohn was doubtful as Zinnemann at that time was regarded as something of an "art-house" director. But he eventually agreed, and the film has the sober realism and narrative skill that one has come to associate with Zinnemann. The action scenes – the knife fight between Prewitt and Fatso Judson (Ernest Borgnine), the vivid reconstruction of Pearl Harbor – are excitingly done; and the portrayal of army life has something of the quality of John Ford, recognizing the need for discipline yet desiring to see that discipline imposed with understanding and sensitivity. The relationships too – the love between Warden and Karen, the friendship between Prewitt and Maggio – seem unconventional, yet convincing and moving. Above all, the defiant character of Prewitt is the conscience of the film and its haunting center of humanity.

From Here to Eternity opened in the summer in New York, generally regarded as a bad time for business. Harry Cohn took out a full page advertisement giving the film his seal of approval, and then sat back nervously awaiting the result of his biggest personal gamble. At midnight in Los Angeles, Zinnemann had a phone call from Marlene Dietrich to tell him that there were queues around the block. "But how do they know? There's been no publicity," said Zinnemann. "They smell it," said Dietrich. It is true that sometimes the public can just sense the possibility of an exceptional film. *From Here to Eternity* did not disappoint their expectations.

Right: *From Here to Eternity* opened at the worst possible time, midsummer in New York, but the passion on the big screen pulled in the audiences. Burt Lancaster is at the center of the story, having an affair **(inset)** with Deborah Kerr, the wife of his C.O. **Below:** *Rebel boxer Montgomery Clift (right) with Sergeant Ernest Borgnine.*

Western
SHANE (Paramount 1953)
GIANT (WB 1956)
Director: George Stevens

Left: *Joey Starrett (Brandon de Wilde) is worried that his hero Shane (played by Alan Ladd) is a coward because he is reluctant to fight; but Shane finally straps on his guns and steps out to take on hired killer Jack Palance* **(above).**

Right: *Success and failure for James Dean. An oil strike brings wealth but not happiness – he becomes increasingly isolated and his love for his neighbor's wife, Elizabeth Taylor,* **below right**, *remains unfulfilled.*

Along with *Duel in the Sun* (1947) and *Butch Cassidy and the Sundance Kid* (1969), *Shane* is one of the most popular westerns ever made. Its immediate novelty for audiences of the time was the splendor of its color, and also its location shooting, which reflected an increasing trend towards realism in the fifties western. But its popularity has endured for many more reasons than that.

The title character is a mysterious gunfighter who rides into a Wyoming valley to find himself caught in the middle of a feud between struggling homesteaders and ruthless ranchers. He cleanses the valley of evil before riding out as mysteriously as he came. The story has the simplicity of myth or legend. Seen through the eyes of a child, it tells of a struggle between Good (personified by Shane) and Evil (personified by the other gunfighter, Wilson) played by Alan Ladd and Jack Palance respectively. In moving towards its suspenseful finale, the film majestically surveys and stylizes all the classic ingredients of a good western: the bar-room brawl, the tense and taunting challenge of a gunfight, the lyrical funeral, the epic final confrontation.

Mythical hero
Shane is a work of elemental power, showing disturbances in Nature when the moral world is awry (as in the thunderstorm that accompanies the gunning down of the homesteader, or in the shot of terrified horses during the fight between Shane and his friend, Joe Starrett). It is also a film of hidden depths, which is the reason that it was critically as well as popularly acclaimed. It shows the contamination of violence and the

dangers as well as the delights of the boy's hero-worship of Shane. There is an implication that Shane stays to help Starrett (Van Heflin) and the homesteaders because he has fallen in love with Starrett's wife, Marion (Jean Arthur), and that she too, frustrated by her existence on the farm, craves for a more romantic life. It is never stated explicitly, but it gives a more subtle, adult perspective to the relationship which widens the film's appeal. The film is perfectly cast. Alan Ladd's performance as Shane was the finest of his career. As a critic put it: "He made mythological amends for his physiological lacks."

Perhaps the main achievement of the film is its discovery of a style that avoids cliché. The plot elements are familiar, but the treatment has such dramatic flair that they are given fresh impact. The soundtrack is used dramatically rather than realistically. A tense whispered conversation between Wilson and his henchmen in the foreground seals the fate of the blustering homesteader in the background; the gunshot that fells him explodes with unnatural loudness; Shane's ritualistic taunt of Wilson seems to resonate from the bowels of the earth; few could forget the echo of the faraway hills in the finale. Warren Beatty has said that he was tremendously influenced by the dramatic use of the soundtrack in *Shane* when he came to produce *Bonnie and Clyde* (1967). The visuals are also astounding. Lingering slow dissolves – of a burning farmhouse and Starrett's flaming anger, of a graveyard and Shane's deadly ride to the town – poetically enlarge the film's emotional expressiveness. It is the directing masterpiece of George Stevens' career.

The James Dean cult

Stevens also had a huge success (and won a directing Oscar) with the modern western, *Giant* (1956). Ostensibly, it is a huge Texas family saga, with the usual dramatic ingredients of wealth, marriage and intolerance. Metaphorically, one can see it as a continuation of *Shane*. It shows the fading of the frontier spirit of old America into the capitalistic ethic of the New. This process is particularly symbolized in the character of Jett Rink, a poor but individualistic cowboy whose discovery of oil turns him into a wealthy but isolated tycoon. Rink was to be the final screen performance of James Dean, whose tragic death in an automobile crash in 1955 triggered a hysteria and cult following that gave an enormous fillip to the success of *Giant*.

The core of the film is actually the relationship between Bick Benedict (Rock Hudson) and his wife Leslie (Elizabeth Taylor). It is through them that we follow the film's themes of generation conflict and social change. Hudson and Taylor have rarely been finer (the former was nominated for an Oscar). But it is Dean whom audiences remember, particularly in those early scenes when he is striding out on his small piece of land, or when he comes to tell Benedict that "my well came in big". He puts his oily hand on one of the white columns of Benedict's porch and, unemphatically, Stevens instantly crystallizes the theme of the film – the muddy thumbprints of materialism on the pillars of elegance and the coming of conflict between the aristocracy and the nouveau riche. "You should have shot that fella a long time ago," a friend says to Benedict about Jett Rink. "Now he's too rich to kill."

Comedy

HOW TO MARRY A MILLIONAIRE (Fox 1953)
Director: Jean Negulesco

THE SEVEN YEAR ITCH (Fox 1955)
Director: Billy Wilder

Reminiscent of a 1946 film, *Three Little Girls in Blue, How To Marry a Millionaire* is a familiar story of three girls who rent an expensive Manhattan apartment and set out to ensnare the richest men they can find. Nothing very original about this, and it is rather colorlessly directed by Jean Negulesco, who had begun his motion picture career in the thirties as, in his own curious words, "technical adviser on a rape scene". Why was the movie so successful?

One can suggest three reasons. It was the first comedy in CinemaScope, which was still a lucrative novelty, and whose width allowed ample opportunity for showing off the sumptuousness of the decor. The title would be an enticement for those who believe that diamonds are still a girl's best friend (the *How To…* film titles of the following decade tend to be even more materialistic and misogynistic: *Murder Your Wife, Succeed in Business Without Really Trying, Steal a Million, Save a Marriage and Ruin Your Life*). The third reason is probably Marilyn Monroe, that gifted comedienne and gorgeous embodiment of innocence who was just becoming an important star. She cannot do much with the part of a wide-eyed simpleton who finally lands David Wayne, but her screen presence is more than equal to that of the ostensible stars, Lauren Bacall and Betty Grable.

Prospect of adultery

Monroe also appeared in the second biggest comedy hit of the fifties, Billy Wilder's *The Seven Year Itch* (1955), also in CinemaScope. This is a much better vehicle for her talents. Left alone in his apartment when his wife and children go off on holiday, a middle-aged New Yorker (Tom Ewell) is tempted by the prospect of an affair with the girl upstairs (Marilyn Monroe). Although it was inevitable that nothing much would happen, the film's mature acknowledgement of the stirrings of adultery appealed to the more broad-minded standards of the time. Ewell is so ordinary, both physically and intellectually, that a male audience could identify with him, while the women in the audience probably enjoyed his ineffectiveness and humiliation.

The main sources of Wilder's humor in the film are: the exuberant sexual imagery, which borders on the rude (skirts above knees, corks jammed in bottles, and the like); the irreverent deployment of the innovations of CinemaScope, Wilder using the extra space to split the screen into separate blocks of reality and fantasy; and the amusing cinematic allusions, which include a parody of the beach scene of *From Here to Eternity*, and the use of Rachmaninov as an appropriate background stimulus for adulterous romance, as in *Brief Encounter* (1945). The film's major attraction is, of course, Monroe.

Symbol of innocence

Actually she is so good that she slightly unbalances the movie, shifting the focus from the yearnings of the hero to the innocent longings of the girl. She plays an actress who appears on toothpaste commercials: "Every time I show my teeth on television, more people see me than ever saw Sarah Bernhardt. It's something to think about, isn't it?" Wilder's disenchantment with a society that can endorse such values is modified by his affection for such characteristic New World naiveté. At this stage of her career, Monroe symbolized that kind of dumb innocence, before stardom and exploitation (in life, as in her films) were to curdle innocence into neurosis. The poignancy is already beginning to overwhelm the comedy by the time of her singing "I'm Through With Love" in Wilder's *Some Like It Hot* (1959), one of the genuinely great comedies of the decade that was also a smash hit.

François Truffaut described Monroe as a graceful cross between Chaplin and James Dean. This implicitly identifies her with the pathos and humor of the former and the problems and youthful self-destructiveness of the latter. "The one thing in Marilyn we can never forget, and perhaps never forgive," said the critic Molly Haskell, "is the painful, naked and embarrassing need for love." One of the funniest moments of *The Seven Year Itch* is, in retrospect, one of the saddest. Ewell's clumsy attempt at seduction ends with him and Monroe on the floor, both having fallen off his piano stool. "I'm dreadfully sorry," he says, scrambling to his feet, "this has never happened to me before." "Oh," Monroe replies brightly, "it happens to me all the time." There would inevitably come a time when the role of sex goddess would no longer be so funny, and the loneliness behind it would become painfully apparent.

Left: *Marilyn Monroe, Betty Grable (center) and Lauren Bacall looking for the elusive millionaire husband.*

Above: *A mischievous subway breeze lifts Marilyn Monroe's skirt and Tom Ewell's hopes,* **below.** *"It happens to me all the time", she reassures him!*

DeMille Epic
THE TEN COMMANDMENTS (Paramount 1956)
THE GREATEST SHOW ON EARTH
(Paramount 1952)
Director: Cecil B. DeMille

"Cecil B. DeMille," said Joseph L. Mankiewicz, disdainfully, "had his finger up the pulse of America." Mankiewicz's simultaneous acknowledgement of the maestro's success and his implied contempt for that achievement encapsulates a common critical response to DeMille. The intelligentsia thought of him as a vulgar showman. Nevertheless, the public loved his blend of spectacle and sermon, and Paramount Pictures had every reason to be grateful to him. According to their figures, by the time of DeMille's death, his films had grossed $750 million for the studio and had been seen by 4,000 million people (excluding television).

DeMille was a man of massive ego and yet supreme humility before the public. His films are a crafty combination of sex, sin and salvation, probably best exemplified by his marketing technique on *Samson and Delilah* (1949), which was sold as a story of faith to mollify the censors but whose lurid pictorialization clearly conformed to DeMille's interpretation of the tale as "for the public, the hottest love story of all time". He was a kind of Victorian story-teller, lecturing his audience on the evils of debauchery but blithely ensuring through his salacious imagery that they knew exactly what the sins of the flesh looked like.

DeMille's taste was completely at one with the decade's preference for blockbuster movies. His big top film, *The Greatest Show on Earth* (1952), was a smash hit and won an Oscar as Best Film of the year. It had DeMille's usual canny mixture of popular elements: daring circus acts to provide excitement; an interesting new star (Charlton Heston); an old star in a different role (James Stewart as a clown, who is also a doctor on the run); and, above all, a set-piece spectacular, which, in this case, is a train crash to end all train crashes.

Virtue triumphant
The Ten Commandments (1956) is even more spectacular and was even more successful. In his silent version of 1923, DeMille had used the biblical story only as a prologue to a modern variation on the theme. But in the fifties' era of Biblical extravaganzas, DeMille tells his version of the whole story. It features a star-crammed cast (Charlton Heston, Yul Brynner, Edward G. Robinson, Vincent Price) and has DeMille himself appearing in a prologue to inform us that, because of the film's length, he has granted us an intermission. Whether directing a crowd of 8 000 people, reconstructing the Calf of Gold orgy or parting the Red Sea, DeMille is in his element, the commanding general organizing his forces on a massive scale to assert the ultimate triumph of virtue.

Secret of his success
Quite apart from the mixture of morality and mayhem, solemnity and sex, DeMille himself thought that the supreme thing in spectacle (and hence the secret of his success) was basically action: fights, chases, confrontations, parades, train crashes, natural disasters. His films give an audience so

Above: *Hollywood's lavish version of* **The Ten Commandments.**

Right: *Moses (Charlton Heston) hands over the leadership of the Jewish people to Joshua (John Derek), with the approval of his wife, Sephora (Yvonne de Carlo). After 40 years in the wilderness, Moses was permitted by God to see the Promised Land but not to enter it. He died at the age of 120. The script of the film, based on four biblical books, Exodus, Leviticus, Numbers, Deuteronomy, was by Aeneas Mackenzie, Jesse Lasky Jr, Jack Gariss, Fred Frank.*

much to look at that it can never rest, and he knows how to fill the frame.

He also knew how to tell a story. "For a long time I thought what he did was a big joke, just preposterous, and I couldn't understand why the audience went for it in such a big way," said George Cukor of DeMille. "The eroticism was a joke. Then I saw *The Ten Commandments*: it was preposterous from the word go ... but the story-telling was wonderful – you were riveted to your seat." DeMille had a gift which even some great directors have never had: a natural narrative sense. When he told a story, an audience might not believe it, but something in the way he told it compelled the audience to hear him out to the finish.

DeMille died in 1959 and, in a way, so did the kind of cinema he represented. "The epic had become demonstrations of what a studio could do, they were the last grand flings of those factories of illusion," said the critic Michael Wood. Behind them was a hope that a film costing this much would in itself persuade the public that it must be worth seeing. DeMille not only believed it: he had throughout his career demonstrated it. His death at the end of the decade signalled the effective end of the epic era. The epics which followed in the early sixties were essentially the death throes of the genre and significantly concentrated on defeat *(Spartacus)*, death *(El Cid)*, disintegration *(Cleopatra)* and decay *(The Fall of the Roman Empire)*.

Below: *Charlton Heston, in only his second Hollywood role (and in modern clothes) as the circus big-top boss in **The Greatest Show on Earth**.* **Right:** *Dorothy Lamour (not in a sarong, for once) lends some glamor to the ring as a showgirl.*

Adventure
AROUND THE WORLD IN 80 DAYS
(Todd-UA 1956)
Director: Michael Anderson

"When he gambles," said a friend of Mike Todd, "he loses racetracks." Todd was the husband of Elizabeth Taylor and a showman on the grand scale. As a conman, by all accounts, he went off the scale altogether. A producer has said that Todd "walked through stone walls" to produce *Around the World in 80 Days*.

The movie is partly epic comedy, in a manner that anticipates Stanley Kramer's *It's a Mad, Mad, Mad, Mad World* (1963), and partly a kind of upmarket package holiday. Jules Verne's story of Phileas Fogg's global sprint provides the flimsiest pretense to exploit various locations (Paris, the temples of Rangoon, Mount Fujiyama) and introduce star-studded cameos in support of David Niven as Fogg. Indeed, the film's main fun comes from identifying the stars. These include Buster Keaton as a railway conductor, Beatrice Lillie as a Salvationist, John Gielgud as Phileas Fogg's valet, Ronald Colman as an Indian railway official, and Trevor Howard as an occupant of Fogg's London club.

Todd talked stars like Sinatra and Dietrich into appearing in the film for a fraction of their normal price by casting Noel Coward first and attracting the rest on the strength of Coward's name. For the Latin-American audience, he cast the popular Mexican comedian Cantinflas in the role of Fogg's new valet and companion, Passepartout.

It would be unfair to give the impression that the movie was a wholly exploitative enterprise. Todd went to extravagant lengths to achieve what he wanted. According to David Niven's autobiography, *The Moon's a Balloon*, these lengths included outwitting the Paris police in shooting on location and stealing a shot of guardsmen in London with a camera concealed in a vegetable barrow. The movie is at its best when it is airborne and making full use of its wide-screen opportunities, particularly in the section when Fogg and Passepartout set out on the second part of their journey in a balloon. They drift over Paris, past the Notre Dame, the French countryside, all magically caught in the vast expanse of Todd-AO; and, in the movie's most cheerful image, Cantinflas scoops some snow from the top of an Alpine mountain to chill a bottle of champagne.

Maiden in distress

Around the World was scripted by S. J. Perelman, James Poe and John Farrow (who was originally scheduled to direct), and shows in places a witty and acute understanding of Jules Verne's novel, especially Verne's observation of Fogg's xenophobia (his reason for traveling the world is not to broaden his outlook but merely to settle a bet made in an English club!). Throughout his world tour in the film, Fogg never once comments on his surroundings and hardly ever looks out of his train window. At one stage, when contemplating whether to rescue an Indian maiden (Shirley MacLaine!), he is told that she had been given an English education. "That settles it," he says and decides on a plan of action. The amiable satire on stuffy Britishness is enhanced by David Niven's starchy yet dignified performance as Fogg, and by composer Victor Young's amusing variations on "Rule Britannia" in his score.

One should not forget the score, the last completed by Victor Young before his death in 1956. The film's main theme was hugely popular and widely recorded, and undoubtedly assisted the movie in attracting its audience. In fact, the technical credits are all excellent (the photography of Lionel Lindon, the art direction of James Sullivan and Ken Adam, the end titles of Saul Bass) and the movie went on to win five Oscars, including Best Picture. Sadly, it turned out to be Mike Todd's testament, for he died in a plane crash in 1958.

Right: *"Sir, you are an insolent bully and I demand satisfaction at once." Phileas Fogg (David Niven) finds that railroad journeys in the Wild West are not without hazard when he encounters a gunfighter (John Carradine).*

Below: *Fogg and his valet Passepartout (Cantinflas) set off on another stage of their great journey. For David Niven (1910-83) the film was just one episode in a long and variable career. For Cantinflas, it was a bid for international stardom that sadly ended in the failure* **Pepe** *(1960).*

Melodrama
PEYTON PLACE (Fox 1957)
Director: Mark Robson

Peyton Place is the name of a small town in New England: it is also a state of mind. Because of Grace Metalious's best-selling novel, Peyton Place had come to be recognized as a site of hypocrisy, prurience and sexual frustration. The action within this setting includes illegitimacy, frigidity and rape, and concludes with a murder trial. In adapting the novel for the screen, the movie makes no claim to be expressing something fundamental about existence, but it does effectively duplicate the appeal of the book – that is, it provides glossy gossip of a high order.

From Here to Eternity had shown that it was possible to imply tempestuous passion without showing anything very much; and *Peyton Place* talks about salacious books and nude sunbathing while remaining visually discreet. It gives off an aura of delicious scandal and implies a community transformed into a seething cauldron of sexuality but it scrupulously avoids providing any offending visual evidence.

Peyton Place also picks up two inter-related strands in popular fifties cinema and exploits them very skilfully. It has elements of the problem picture, in which the troubles of the younger generation could be related to tensions within the family. It is also part of Hollywood's flourishing fifties melodrama cycle which allowed films, within certain limits, to tackle subject matter that was too hot to handle on television.

Welcome to Maine

Peyton Place does not have the delirious extremes of melodrama in the hands of masters like Douglas Sirk (*All That Heaven Allows, Written on the Wind* and *Imitation of Life*) and Vincente Minnelli (*The Cobweb, Lust for Life, Tea and Sympathy*). But it does have two useful ironic strategies up its sleeve. The grubby emotions and ignoble behavior of the community are effectively counterpointed with the natural settings of countryside and woods against which the drama takes place. An even more striking contrast is provided by the emphasis on the community's religious devotions, which heightens the split between outward pious display and inward passionate yearning. This particular element in the film led to a certain amount of difficulty. The original intention had been to shoot the film in Woodstock, Vermont but, because of pressure from some of the town's church groups, the idea had to be abandoned. "Please come to Maine where we are broadminded," telegraphed the Governor to director Mark Robson, on hearing of his difficulty, which is what Robson did.

The cast are especially well chosen, and the Oscar-nominated performers (Lana Turner, Arthur Kennedy, Hope Lange and Diane Varsi) have rarely acquitted themselves better on screen. Franz Waxman's score is attractive, and it is small wonder that the film inspired a sequel (*Return to Peyton Place*) and a successful television series. In fact, the melodrama of life was to imitate that of fiction when, within a year of *Peyton Place*, Lana Turner's daughter stabbed to death her mother's lover. The reason for the enormous publicity generated by the inquest into the case is probably not very different from the enormous success of *Peyton Place*: there is nothing the public relishes more than star-studded scandal.

Some of Hollywood's most successful films in the fifties were centered around the family, revealing its tensions and teenage anxiety. Allison, **left and right**, temporarily forgets hers until Mum (Lana Turner), **above**, takes a hand. Lana Turner is hoping that the adage "Like mother, like daughter" won't turn out to be true since Allison is illegitimate.

War

THE BRIDGE ON THE RIVER KWAI
(Columbia 1957)
Director: David Lean

"Man came into this world to build, not to destroy," said producer Sam Spiegel when talking about the main theme of his film, *The Bridge on the River Kwai*. "Yet he's thrown into the necessity of destroying, and his one everlasting instinct is to try and save himself from having to destroy."

The film deals with the situation of British prisoners of war who are ordered to build a bridge to accommodate the Burma-Siam railway. Their instinct is to sabotage the bridge but, under the leadership of Colonel Nicholson (Alec Guinness), they are persuaded that the bridge should be constructed as a symbol of British morale, spirit and dignity in adverse circumstances. Unknown to them, the Allies have sent a mission into the jungle, led by Warden (Jack Hawkins) and an American, Shears (William Holden), to blow up the bridge.

The film reunited actor Alec Guinness with director David Lean after their successful association together on Lean's classic Dickens adaptations of the forties, *Great Expectations* (1946) and *Oliver Twist* (1948). Guinness was at first reluctant to play the main role. He thought Nicholson "a blinkered character. I wondered how we could get audiences to take him seriously." The film initially encourages sympathy for Nicholson when he bravely endures torture rather than compromise his principles for the benefit of the Japanese commandant Saito (Sessue Hayakawa). Guinness's performance gives tremendous conviction to an honorable but arrogant man, who is slowly revealed to be a deluded obsessive. He convinces himself that the bridge is a monument to British character, but actually it is a monument to himself, and his insistence on its construction becomes a subtle form of collaboration with the enemy.

In an unexpected way, all the three main characters betray themselves. Warden seems an example of British moderation and fair play, but he reveals himself as blinkered and as morally confused as Nicholson. Shears probes and questions the motivations of everyone involved, but he too is forced into the role of reluctant hero. The film builds to a memorably messy finale in which all the tensions, obsessions and contradictions collide with each other and then explode into utter confusion.

Battered reputation

The film is a study of the madness of war, and can be taken also as a black comedy about inflexible military attitudes. David Lean was obviously attracted both to the peculiar madness of the hero and the challenge of the landscape – two recurrent aspects of his films that are continued in his next film, *Lawrence of Arabia* (1962). With *The Bridge on the River Kwai*, he became the first British director ever to win a Hollywood Oscar.

The film was vastly acclaimed at the time, which certainly enhanced its box-office prospects, although over the years its reputation has come in for something of a battering. Some feel it obscures its anti-war theme through its simultaneous presentation of war as an exciting adventure, while many have commented on the obscurity of the ending (does Nicholson accidentally or intentionally fall on the dynamite

detonator?). But the fact that it has provoked a wide range of comment and discussion is probably one of the reasons for its enduring appeal. Unusually for a film of this scope, the characters are not swamped by the budget or by the locale. Also they are distinctly odd and unusual, constantly pulling themselves and the story in unexpected directions. Lean has always been one of the masters of film narrative. With *Kwai*, he attached this gift to a tragic, ironic, sometimes farcical study of character, a combination that impressed both the public and the press.

Shears (played by William Holden), the escaped American prisoner of war, reluctantly agrees to aid British commando Major Warden (Jack Hawkins) in blowing up the railroad bridge that his fellow prisoners are building for the Japanese in Siam.

Musical
SOUTH PACIFIC (Magna/Fox 1958)
Director: Joshua Logan

South Pacific was the fourth Rodgers and Hammerstein musical to be made into a major film in four years (the previous three being *Oklahoma!* in 1955 and *Carousel* and *The King and I* in 1956). It was clearly felt that large-scale musicals were a film form particularly suited to a wide-screen format that could show off exotic places. Made in Todd-AO and shot extensively on location on the island of Kauai and the Fiji Islands, *South Pacific* was a colossal hit.

Josh Logan seemed especially good casting for *South Pacific*; he had co-written and directed the successful stage version in 1949. He also co-wrote and directed the stage version of *Mister Roberts* the previous year, which was to be made into a highly successful film in 1955, and was also about naval life on the fringes of the war in the Pacific. When he came to direct the screen version of *South Pacific*, Logan and the cameraman Leon Shamroy had certain ideas about how the film should look, not all of which coincided. Logan insisted on color filters for the songs to contribute to a particular mood: soft purple for "Younger than Springtime", yellow for "Cockeyed Optimist" and multi-colored for "Bali Ha'i" to suggest an island of wish-fulfilment. Shamroy was especially unhappy with the latter sequence. He had wanted to shoot on actual tropical locations and with animation effects, but the producers overruled his ideas and used a painted backdrop for Bali Ha'i. Later Josh Logan was to say to a friend: "Tell Leon he was right about opposing the filters in *South Pacific* ... but also tell him I made three million dollars out of that movie."

Mystery success
Logan himself has admitted that the enormous success of the film (it ran in one of London's biggest cinemas for over four years) has always mystified him. Clearly the very attractive score would bring in the loyal Rodgers and Hammerstein fans (certainly the record sales of the soundtrack album were prodigious). The movie would attract an audience aware of its Broadway success, and it would exploit its blockbuster status with the customary prestige packaging and heavy publicity that had proved so successful during the decade. The dramatic element in the movie might also have pulled in people who were not necessarily fans of the usual escapism of musicals. Although providing ample scope for comedy (notably during "There ain't nothin' like a dame", with Ray Walston and the sailors prancing like caged lions), *South Pacific* had a basically serious main theme. An American nurse (Mitzi Gaynor) falls in love with a French planter (Rossano Brazzi) who has some Polynesian children from a previous marriage. The racial tension between them is echoed when an American sailor (John Kerr) also falls in love with a Polynesian girl (France Nuyen).

The theme of miscegenation and racial harmony had been examined by Logan in his previous film, *Sayonara* (1957), which had criticized the attitude of the American army to mixed marriages. The viewpoint of *South Pacific* is liberal, but without really challenging anyone's prior prejudices, since the American sailor is killed and there seem to be no racial grounds whatever why Mitzi Gaynor should not finally marry Rossano Brazzi. By making the theme palatable, the movie makes it profitable as well. The dramatic material provides a solid context for songs like "Happy Talk" and "Some Enchanted Evening" but the unreal style keeps it on the level of fantasy. Interestingly, Fred Zinnemann thought his film of *Oklahoma!* had failed in relative terms because he made it too realistic: Judd (Rod Steiger) was supposed to be a stage villain yet he came over as a psychologically complex and interesting character. For all the dramatic tensions and racial undercurrents, there is no complexity in *South Pacific*, and no place where it really impinges on an audience's social conscience. You can think about the issues but take reassurance from the fact that it seems all to be taking place in a land of fantasy – a Bali Ha'i of the mind.

Above: *Emile de Becque (Rossano Brazzi) hopes that one enchanted evening his American nurse will agree to marry him but Nellie Forbush (Mitzi Gaynor — **right**), though in love with a wonderful guy, is a cockeyed optimist if she thinks he will trust her with the truth about his Polynesian half-caste children.*

Epic
BEN-HUR (MGM 1959)
Director: William Wyler

Reputed to be the worst American novel ever written, General Lew Wallace's *Ben-Hur* had been a best-seller since its first publication in 1880. One might remember that Humphrey Bogart's Philip Marlowe is pretending to be looking for a special edition of that novel in the famous bookstore scene of *The Big Sleep* (1946). Wallace's Victorian combination of the sacred and the profane in his story might be said to anticipate DeMille. *Ben-Hur* is basically a melodrama, with violence and piety combined in a story that cleverly parallels the life of Christ with that of a more active hero who is flawed but also sympathetic and dynamic.

In the twenties, *Ben-Hur* had been one of MGM's most spectacular, costly and successful films. It is not surprising that during the fifties, when the studio was going through the worst period in its history (in 1957, it had incurred a loss for the first time ever), MGM should return to *Ben-Hur* for box-office inspiration. It was in the popular blockbuster mode, and the studio could use the recently developed Camera 65 process for brightly defined wide-screen images. However, the choice of director would be crucial. MGM chose the experienced and brilliant William Wyler to take charge of his first epic.

Oscar record
Ironically, one of Wyler's first jobs in the industry had been as an assistant in the silent version of *Ben-Hur*, helping to organize the extras in the crowd scenes for the chariot race. However, this had no real bearing on his selection now. Indeed, the pulsating chariot race sequence of the new version was mainly put into the hands of the second unit, led by Andrew Marton, and the sea battle was handled by a third unit, led by Richard Thorpe. It was felt the action elements of the film could take care of themselves. Wyler's job was to bring his taste and skill as a co-ordinator of talents to the human drama, and to give the production an aura of artistry quite different from the tub-thumping showmanship of DeMille. He succeeded so well that the film's total of eleven Oscars – including Best Film, Best Director, Actor (Charlton Heston), Supporting Actor (Hugh Griffith), music, photography – has yet to be surpassed.

The one Oscar the film did not win was for its screenplay, which is ironic but understandable. Ironic, because it is an unusually literate and poetic piece of writing and conveys the character conflicts superbly. Understandable, because there was a lot of confusion over the precise credits. Karl Tunberg is the credited contributor, but poet and playwright Christopher Fry also supplies deft phrases to suggest the style and period of the piece. Gore Vidal worked on the relationship between the two former friends, the Jewish prince, Judah Ben-Hur (Heston) and the Roman commander, Messala (Stephen Boyd), planting a suspicion that the latter's brutality towards the hero and his family subconsciously stems from a feeling of unrequited love. Stephen Boyd was also passed over by the Academy, but his performance as Messala contains the finest acting of his career.

Although undoubtedly stirred by the battling boats and surging chariots, audiences were also deeply moved by the

Above: *Charlton Heston as Judah Ben-Hur had to learn to drive a chariot for the thrilling climactic race.*

personal drama. Unlike DeMille, the sexuality of the movie is relatively subdued, and some of the strongest scenes are those involving the Christ story, as in the moment when Christ gives Ben-Hur some water in the desert, or the imposing and brutal reconstruction of the Crucifixion. The characterization contains some fascinating subtleties, paradoxes and violent shifts. Ben-Hur's best friend suddenly becomes his worst enemy, forcing him into the role of victimized Jew; and then his fiercest foe, the Roman commander Arrius (Jack Hawkins), becomes a devoted substitute-father, forcing him into the role of triumphant Roman. Ben-Hur's fluctuating identity adds additional tension to his dilemma as a basically pacifist figure filled with thoughts of revenge.

Pacifism and revenge were themes that preoccupied Wyler at this time, in movies such as *The Desperate Hours* (1955), *Friendly Persuasion* (1956) and *The Big Country* (1958). For Wyler, *Ben-Hur* was not a quaint period piece. Its story of the struggle of the Jews for their freedom still had contemporary relevance. His identification with the story touched modern audiences in a way that few previous epics had done, and the movie continues to be successfully revived.

CHAPTER FOUR:

THE SIXTIES

With the continuing decline in audiences, all the major American companies began to diversify into other areas of leisure entertainment in the sixties: records, publishing and the production of filmed television series and TV movies. More films were shot abroad to take advantage of the lower costs. There was a great increase in filming in Britain, stimulated by the success of international productions like *The Guns of Navarone* (1961) and *Lawrence of Arabia* (1962). The international success of other British movies also had an impact on film tastes and product in America. The popularity of *Dr No* in 1962 (the first of the James Bond cycle) stimulated a rash of secret agent movies that emulated the Bond movies' adroit blend of sex and spying. The smash hit period comedy *Tom Jones* (1963) took everyone by surprise. It showed that a freshly thought out approach to literary classics could still yield dividends at the box-office: *Doctor Zhivago* (1965), *A Man for All Seasons* (1966) and *Romeo and Juliet* (1968) were to be further examples of this trait. *Tom Jones* also showed the appeal of a bawdy, bouncy attitude to sex.

The naughty but nice material of *Irma La Douce* (1963) had a similar appeal. Reflecting a more permissive era in the movies, the sex comedy was brought stylishly into the heart of mainstream cinema with the Woody Allen scripted *What's New Pussycat?* (1965) and Paul Mazursky's saucy wife-swapping satire, *Bob & Carol & Ted & Alice* (1969). Comedy flourished too with Disney's *The Love Bug* (1968).

Right: *In **Lawrence of Arabia** (1962) Sherif Ali (Omar Sharif) rides out of a mirage to shoot down Lawrence's guide at a water-hole. After this violent introduction, it is not surprising that Ali's tribal possessiveness extends to driving out the Turks and he joins Lawrence in taking the port of Aqaba. (Omar Sharif was nominated for an Oscar on his debut in non-Egyptian films.)*

Top right: *Fashion editor Michael James (Peter O'Toole) attempts to outstrip sexy but suicidal stripper Liz (Paula Prentiss) in one of the sixties' revolutionary hits, **What's New Pussycat?** (1965).*

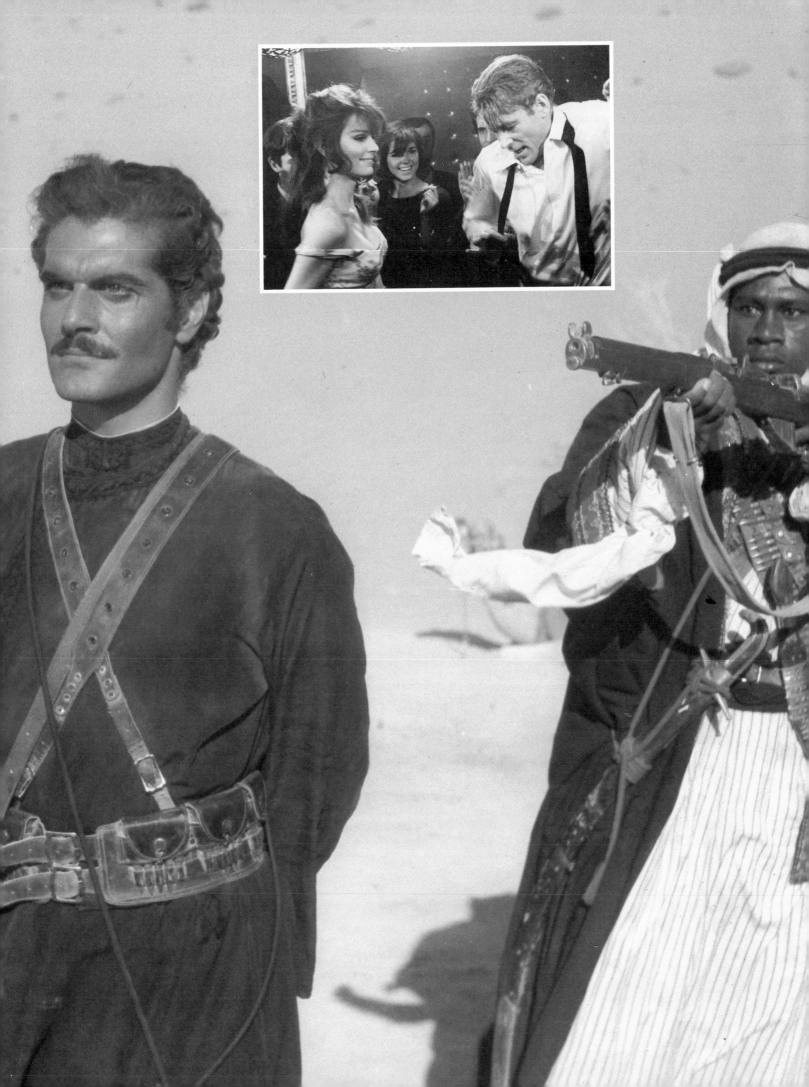

The permissive sixties revitalized Hollywood's attitude to sex as seen here in the swashbuckling **Tom Jones** *(1963),* **top***; with the naughty but nice* **Irma La Douce** *(1963),* **right***; and the wife-swapping antics of* **Bob & Carol & Ted & Alice** *(1969),* **(below)***.*

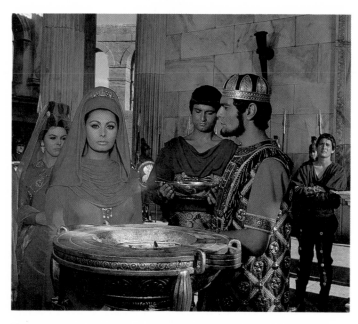

*The blockbuster epic lived on into the sixties, relying on big stars and big subjects. Here Sophia Loren appears in **El Cid** (1961), (above); trainee gladiator **Spartacus** (1960) – played by Kirk Douglas – is selected for a fight to the death (right); and the Allies set about the Nazis in the invasion of June 6 1944, **The Longest Day** (1962), produced by Darryl F. Zanuck (inset).*

Fall of the epic

One legacy from the fifties that did not flourish in the subsequent decade was the blockbuster epic. Some examples of the genre were quite distinguished and fared well enough commercially, like *Spartacus* (1960) and *El Cid* (1961). But costly productions like the 1962 MGM remake of *Mutiny on the Bounty* (with a temperamental Marlon Brando as Christian and a rapidly changing personnel of writers and directors) failed to recoup their investment. Samuel Bronston's productions of *55 Days at Peking* (1963) and *The Fall of the Roman Empire* (1964) were expensive flops. The failure of George Stevens' painstaking *The Greatest Story Ever Told* (1965) signalled the twilight of a distinguished career: he was to make only one more film. Fox's traumatic production of *Cleopatra* (1963) echoed the Roman Empire itself in its self-destructive gargantuanism.

New wave in Hollywood

After a disastrous period between 1961 and 1963, all of the major companies had more or less recovered by the middle of the decade, at which point the industry was transformed by a wave of mergers and take-overs. In his book, *Growing Up in Hollywood*, Robert Parrish tells of a party he attended for Charles Bluhdorn, the head of a conglomerate called Gulf and Western that had taken over Paramount. Noticing at one stage that Bluhdorn was surrounded by twenty-five men with all the women in the room left unattended, Mrs Sam Goldwyn observed drily to Parrish: "New girl in town." In the new industrial structure of Hollywood, the money and the power were to lie with these conglomerates. Control of Universal was transferred to MCA. United Artists was taken over by Transamerica Corporation. Warner Brothers, first merged with Seven Arts, finally ended up as part of the Kinney National Corporation, with the entire company rechristened Warner Communications Inc. in 1970.

Of all the ups and downs experienced by the film companies during the sixties, none reflects the cyclical uncertainties and unpredictable tastes of the period more than Fox. Darryl F. Zanuck took charge of *The Longest Day* (1962), his massive reconstruction of the Allied landings in Normandy, and his faith and vision were rewarded at the box-office. But the gains from that were almost entirely wiped out by the nerve-racking experience of *Cleopatra*.

From the brink of bankruptcy, the studio was rescued by *The Sound of Music* (1965), which was the most rampaging box-office smash since *Gone with the Wind*. But another large-scale musical, *Doctor Dolittle* (1967), designed to cash in on the success of *The Sound of Music*, was a financial fiasco, as was the Julie Andrews film, *Star!* (1968). So also was *Tora! Tora! Tora!* (1969), Fox's attempt to do for Pearl Harbor what *The Longest Day* had done for D-Day. At the same time, a film in which the company had very little faith, *Planet of the Apes* (1968), was second only to *2001: A Space Odyssey* (1968), as the most financially successful fantasy film of the decade.

The Sound of Music has a lot to answer for. Earlier musicals of the decade, such as *West Side Story* (1961) and *My Fair Lady* (1964) had done modestly well at the box-office, and the Disney musical fantasy *Mary Poppins* (1964) had been especially popular. After *The Sound of Music*, however, all the major studios were looking to the musical to revive their fortunes, and in most cases they did not succeed and most of them did not deserve to. The star of the biggest hit of the decade, Julie Andrews, was also the star of some of the biggest flops: *Hawaii* (1966), *Star!*, *Darling Lili* (1970). The musical actress who made the most successful debut of the late sixties was Barbra Streisand in *Funny Girl* (1968), winning an Oscar for her portrayal of Fanny Brice. *Oliver!* (1968), based on Charles Dickens' novel *Oliver Twist*, was another of the most successful musicals of this decade.

Freedom of expression

At the other end of the scale from *The Sound of Music*, the virtual abolition of film censorship in the United States led to new freedoms of language and subject matter and a more explicit treatment of sex and violence. Richard Burton and Elizabeth Taylor raged their way through a fine adaptation of Edward Albee's raw dissection of a marriage, *Who's Afraid of Virginia Woolf?* (1966). (Parenthetically, as a sign of the times, the large fees from the sale of film rights to color television meant the virtual end of filming in black and white, and *Virginia Woolf* was the last major monochrome box-office hit of the decade.)

Above: *"He was a great big fat flop!"* Elizabeth Taylor as Martha vindictively sums up the academic career of husband George (Richard Burton) in the crackling success **Who's Afraid of Virginia Woolf?** (1966).

Left: *The Sound of Music* (1965) was the perfect vehicle for governess Maria (Julie Andrews), who sings away all known family tensions and Nazi opposition as she leads seven spellbound children over the Alps to a bright new future.

Right: Box-office star Barbra Streisand made her movie debut as Fanny Brice, the vaudeville singing star of the early twenties, in **Funny Girl** (1968) and shared an Oscar for Best Actress with Katharine Hepburn.

Traditional genres, like the gangster, the thriller, the war film, the horror film, the western, became increasingly graphic in their portrayal of violence. *Bonnie and Clyde* (1967) and *Bullitt* (1968) soaked the crime film in blood. In the sixties western, Ford and Hawks had paid tribute to the aging heroes of the past in *The Man Who Shot Liberty Valance* (1962) and *El Dorado* (1967), respectively, and John Wayne at last won an Oscar for his ripe performance as the rascally marshal in *True Grit* (1969). But the most potent western hero of the Sixties was Clint Eastwood, the man with no name – and few honorable values – in the savage spaghetti westerns of Sergio Leone, *A Fistful of Dollars* (1964), *For a Few Dollars More* (1965) and *The Good, the Bad and the Ugly* (1966). The most resonant western director of the decade was Sam Peckinpah. The slow-motion killings of Peckinpah's *The Wild Bunch* (1969) signalled the ending of the elegiac western and dragged the genre, kicking and screaming, into our brutal modern age.

As always, Hollywood was cautious in assimilating into its product the mood of American society. The sixties was a turbulent social decade, dominated by political assassination, youth protest, permissive sexuality, anti-authoritarian attitudes, and a rumbling disquiet over the war in Vietnam. The elderly and conservative film industry circled warily around these trends. Its liberalism and social analysis did not extend much further than sweet pieces about racial harmony like *In the Heat of the Night* (1967) and *Guess Who's Coming to Dinner* (1967). But Hollywood had to take heed when a younger audience and changing tastes began to have its effect on their takings. The enormous profits from relatively inexpensive youth ventures like *Easy Rider* (1969) and *Woodstock* (1969) presaged the dawn of a new age in Hollywood. For the first time since *Citizen Kane*, directing a film was to become a young man's profession.

Left: *The Wild Bunch.*
Above: *Easy Rider.*
Opposite top: *Guess Who's Coming to Dinner.*
Opposite below: *The Good, the Bad and the Ugly.*
Below: *In the Heat of the Night.*

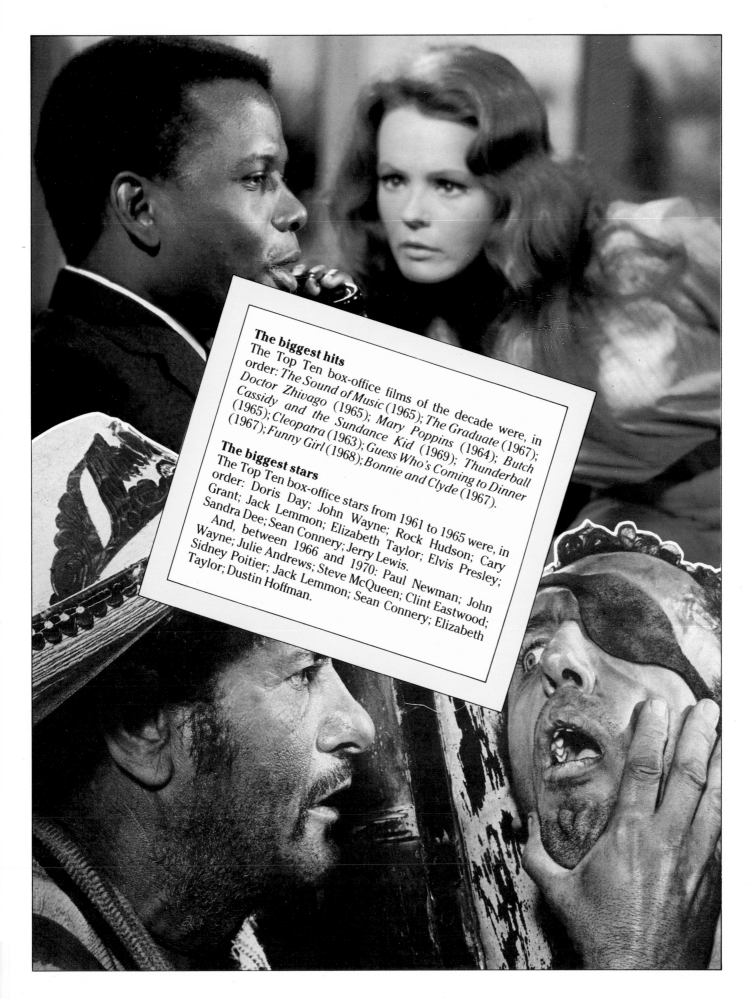

The biggest hits
The Top Ten box-office films of the decade were, in order: *The Sound of Music* (1965); *The Graduate* (1967); *Doctor Zhivago* (1965); *Mary Poppins* (1964); *Butch Cassidy and the Sundance Kid* (1969); *Thunderball* (1965); *Cleopatra* (1963); *Guess Who's Coming to Dinner* (1967); *Funny Girl* (1968); *Bonnie and Clyde* (1967).

The biggest stars
The Top Ten box-office stars from 1961 to 1965 were, in order: Doris Day; John Wayne; Rock Hudson; Cary Grant; Jack Lemmon; Elizabeth Taylor; Elvis Presley; Sandra Dee; Sean Connery; Jerry Lewis. And, between 1966 and 1970: Paul Newman; John Wayne; Julie Andrews; Steve McQueen; Clint Eastwood; Sidney Poitier; Jack Lemmon; Sean Connery; Elizabeth Taylor; Dustin Hoffman.

Horror
PSYCHO (Paramount 1960)
Director: Alfred Hitchcock

With *Psycho*, Alfred Hitchcock took his biggest risk and had his biggest success. The risk was not financial. *Psycho* was a comparatively cheap film to make – it cost less than a million dollars – and was shot quickly by Hitchcock, using the cameraman, John L. Russell, with whom he had worked on his popular television series. However, there was considerable risk in the subject matter. The film was about a deranged split personality. If the public and the press had found it distasteful, the careers of actor Anthony Perkins (who played the role) and Hitchcock could have suffered a severe setback.

One need only think of what happened to Billy Wilder's career after the critical outcry over his black comedy, *Kiss Me Stupid* (1964), which has many similarities with *Psycho* (traumatic events at a strange guest house, significant actions around a filling station and shower, a brassiered heroine preparing for an afternoon of love, a similar obsession with money and sex in an America of forbidding gray anonymity). Wilder was to continue to make fine films, but he never recovered his commercial impetus, and the moral censure directed at the film wounded him deeply. Hitchcock had some moralistic brickbats to contend with over *Psycho*, but he could be reassured by the box-office receipts. The movie took twenty times more than it cost.

Three shocks

For Hitchcock, *Psycho* was basically a "fun film", like a ride on a rollercoaster, during which an audience delights in the pleasure of a good fright. Character involvement was less important than the eliciting of a response from an audience through pure technique. The movie is basically structured around three shocks: the murder of the heroine (Janet Leigh) in the shower; the murder of the private detective (Martin Balsam) who is investigating the heroine's disappearance; and the discovery of the (literally) mummified body in the cellar which holds the clue to the identity of the murderer. The biggest shock is the first, coming completely out of the blue. From that point onwards, the movie becomes less horrific but more tense, because the horror has been transferred to the mind of the audience.

The shower murder has become one of the most famous and analyzed of all screen sequences. In terms of visual gore, it is relatively restrained, but the scene has an enormous impact through a variety of causes: the icily effective screaming violins of Bernard Herrmann's score; the fast cutting of the sequence which seems to correspond to the slashing of a knife; and the fact that the victim is not only a star but the character with whom we have been identifying so far in the film. The murder seems to cut the ground from under our feet.

From here our attention is given to the character who discovers the murder, Norman Bates, and Anthony Perkins' performance comes into its own. With characteristic black humor, Hitchcock involves us in the macabre mopping up of the evidence. He delights in that moment when the car seems to stick in the swamp, and an audience suddenly feels apprehensive on behalf of a man who is concealing a murder.

Part of Hitchcock's strategy in his movies was to allow audiences to indulge their impure emotions and then make them sweat because of them. Like the heroine's sister (Vera Miles), we fear what is in that cellar – but nothing could stop us from investigating. When Hitchcock was once asked to define the deepest logic of his films, he replied: "To put the audience through it."

Horror in the family

Yet the success of *Psycho* cannot entirely be defined in terms of audience manipulation. Certainly it was cleverly advertised: Janet Leigh provocatively clad in her white bra; Anthony Perkins with hand over mouth in an expression of horror; Hitchcock (by now an especially well-known personality through his humorous cameos on his television dramas) declaring that no one would be allowed in after the film has started. But there was more. The sweaty love scene that opens the film seemed unusually explicit for Hitchcock (or Hollywood, for that matter), not only underlining the sexual theme that is at the root of the movie, but seeming to angle the material towards a new, younger audience.

For all the sparse attention to the characters, Anthony Perkins and Janet Leigh give the performances of their lives, playing with great sympathy two social and sexual victims whose identities are to be consumed in a bizarre series of events. Behind the technical and narrative mechanisms of the film is a picture of a cold, ruthless, modern age. It locates the roots of horror in the heart of the American family, something that will be picked up later in the decade in Polanski's chilling *Rosemary's Baby* (1968) and pursued through countless horror films in the seventies. It is remarkably outspoken in its treatment of voyeurism and sexual obsession, but its effect is emotional more than immediately intellectual. Because of Hitchcock's cinematic genius, the movie has proved an inexhaustible treasure-trove for cineastes and horror films alike, and his extraordinary imagination has suddenly given a shiver of terror to the most ordinary objects and situations of everyday life. Motels and showers have never seemed quite the same since *Psycho*.

__Psycho__ boasts some of the greatest shocks in the history of the cinema; seemingly innocuous Norman is the kind of man few would want to meet in the shower, and as for his mother…

Musical
THE SOUND OF MUSIC (Argyle/Fox 1965)
Director: Robert Wise

With some reason, 20th Century-Fox had confidence in *The Sound of Music* from the outset. They had a skilled and experienced director in Robert Wise, who, with screenwriter Ernest Lehman, had already displayed a gift with musicals in the award-winning *West Side Story* (1961). In the starring role of the singing governess, they had Julie Andrews, who had won an Oscar for a similar role the previous year in *Mary Poppins*. With these ingredients, plus a hit score from Rodgers and Hammerstein, the studio allowed a generous budget to permit Todd-AO (70mm) filming on location in Salzburg. This took the stagy original into the open air with spectacular effect. Nevertheless, not even Fox could have predicted the scale of the film's success, making *The Sound of Music* far and away the most popular musical ever made.

What was it that attracted so many people to the film, in some cases again and again? Julie Andrews has said that it was the quality of "joy" in the film. The title song, with a helicopter shot emphasizing the scenic grandeur and the heroine's soaring spirit, immediately sets the tone. Throughout the film, even the ordinary songs (like "Do-Re-Mi") gain an extra frisson from the exuberant filming, the cast's high spirits and the awesome settings. Whereas in Rodgers and Hammerstein's *South Pacific* the songs lifted the movie, in *The Sound of Music* the movie lifts the songs. Taking the camera outdoors compensates for the film's absence of choreography.

Based on fact
Like many of the best musicals, *The Sound of Music* has an element of fairytale. Beauty (Julie Andrews) entrances the Beast (Christopher Plummer's Captain von Trapp) away from the clutches of a calculating fairy godmother (Eleanor Parker's Baroness), to the delight of the children. It is the ultimate Utopian structure for the musical, in which love and romance conquer all and dreams really do come true. On top of that, the film has an infallible defense against accusations of saccharine sentiment: the story is true. It can thus go all out in its endeavors to move an audience.

Women might have been especially drawn to the film because it does have a lot to say about their role. The Captain is a disciplinarian whose values are changed and humanized by the warmth and example of the governess whom he has employed and whom he grows to love. She

Above: *Directness, in addition to fresh air, exercise and exploring the countryside around Salzburg are high on the curriculum when Maria (Julie Andrews) takes over the Trapps' education. Immediately she is in conflict with Captain von Trapp (Christopher Plummer), who has much stricter views on education and imposes an inflexible naval discipline on his seven children (**right**). Love, however, is the victor; Trapp proposes (**top right**) to the simple country girl who promptly leads her happy family through the Alps, beyond the Nazis, to safety.*

transforms his domestic tyranny so that the Trapps can become a genuinely democratic family, but she does so without having to sacrifice her independence and femininity.

Feelings in song

It also has much to say about the role of music in people's lives. Every important emotion in the film – love of nature, love of someone, even love of country – is expressed in song and through music. No musical so powerfully vindicates the *importance* of music to every aspect of human existence, so that the sound of music is not simply something that happens when the dialogue stops but is a key theme of the whole movie.

It also has a dramatic story to tell – namely, the escape of the Trapp family across the Austrian Alps from the Nazis. The film gains a certain poignancy from its nostalgia for a disappearing world (as expressed in the song "Edelweiss"). With other Rodgers and Hammerstein musicals like *The King and I* and *South Pacific*, it deals with some of the horrors of intolerance. But it keeps the grim reality of the Nazis at arm's length and the story it tells ultimately shows the triumph of love and music over barbarism. This optimistic, romantic message has always been at the heart of Hollywood practice, and it has rarely been expressed with such cinematic panache as in *The Sound of Music*.

Romance
DOCTOR ZHIVAGO (Ponti/MGM 1965)
Director: David Lean

Left: *Director David Lean on set near Madrid (not Moscow).*
Below: *A brief idyll for Zhivago (Omar Sharif) and Lara (Julie Christie).*
Bottom: *A wretched train ride for Zhivago, his wife (Geraldine Chaplin), son (Jeffrey Rockland) and father-in-law (Ralph Richardson).*

From Tara to Lara. When MGM embarked on the film version of Boris Pasternak's Nobel Prize-winning novel, *Doctor Zhivago*, they must have hoped that it would emulate the unparalleled success of *Gone with the Wind*. To their mind, it had similar ingredients: a tragic love story, set against the massive background of war, separation and reconstruction. In the event, they were proved right. *Zhivago* was not a success on the scale of *Gone with the Wind* – that would have been beyond expectation – but it certainly brought in audiences time and again to enjoy the spectacle and the passion.

Director David Lean's two previous movies had been the immensely successful *The Bridge on the River Kwai* and *Lawrence of Arabia*. In these he had demonstrated his skill in coping with foreign locations, and with long and complex narratives, whilst at the same time keeping the human story at the forefront of the frame. All these qualities are crucial to the success of *Zhivago*. *Kwai* and *Lawrence* had basically been stories about men, in which women had played hardly any part. *Zhivago* was the chance for Lean to do a really romantic film, for which he was eminently well qualified. Had he not directed the most moving love story in the British cinema, *Brief Encounter* (1945)?

Terror and repose

Zhivago is a series of brief encounters – between the poet Zhivago (Omar Sharif), his loved one Lara (Julie Christie), his half-brother (Alec Guinness), the villainous sensualist Komarovsky (Rod Steiger), and the student Pasha who will become the revolutionary Strelnikoff (Tom Courtenay). The fates of these characters are bounced against the brutality of history in the Russia of the early twentieth century. Lean holds the narrative together with splendid skill, equally at home whether showing the murdering Cossacks, the terrifying train journey or moments of repose when spring breaks through the snow and when Zhivago writes his love poems by candlelight.

The connecting thread is Zhivago's love for Lara. It was the love story that appealed to Lean, and he feels that it is basically the wonderful love story at the core of the film that attracted audiences. More specifically, it is probably Lara, more than Zhivago, who gives the film its power, because her fate is more complex and moving. Omar Sharif's brown eyes are much used for expressive effect, but he does not suggest the soul of a poet. But Julie Christie's radiant Lara certainly suggests the inspiration for the poetry. Also her dilemma is so much more compelling than Zhivago's. She is the former fiancée of Strelnikoff; a woman who has belonged both to beast (Komarovsky) and poet (Zhivago); and a woman who can haunt and entrance even a severe military man (Guinness's Zevgraf). She is last seen disappearing down a street dominated by a huge poster of Stalin – implicitly to become one of the victims of the later purges. Maurice Jarre's "Lara's Theme" became a popular hit, and it is Lara, not Zhivago, who is the *theme* of the film, its heart and its soul.

Thriller
THUNDERBALL (Eon/UA 1965)
Director: Terence Young

After a surfeit of social realism, the James Bond films brought an affluent, amoral adventurism to the British cinema, all decked out in gaudy color. Ian Fleming's novels had started acquiring a cult following during the fifties. They were praised by thriller writers such as Raymond Chandler and known as the favorite light reading of John F. Kennedy. They were also attacked by critics and educationalists for what was seen as a crude combination of sex, snobbery and sadism. It was obvious that such popular texts would find their way to the cinema, but what was important was the timing and the tone.

The early Bond films – *Dr No* (1962), *From Russia with Love* (1963), *Goldfinger* (1964) – emerged in the middle of the international impact of British cinema and the whole ethos of "Swinging England". By casting a poised and ironic Sean Connery in the role, the series avoided the snobbery of the books, in keeping with the more egalitarian spirit of the times. But they did exploit the sexual element, Bond's cool promiscuity seeming to harmonize with the more open sexual morality of the age.

Girls and gadgets
The formula of the Bond series was set almost immediately and has varied very little over the years. A stylish pre-credit sequence establishes the scene and the tone. The credits have a fancy design by Maurice Binder and a title song sung by a popular recording artist of the time. Thereafter, it is a combination of stunts and girls. Bond is ironical towards his boss M (this is more marked in the Connery movies and echoes the sixties' distrust of authority and elders). However, Bond's mettle is tested by having to oppose a master criminal who is generally threatening some form of world domination. In the meantime, Bond is tempted by two females, one of whom is true, the other treacherous, and these relationships give him the opportunity to release some dubious double-entendres. The other constant element is the technical gadgetry which surrounds Bond and is deployed by him for protection and to show his technical expertise.

As the series blossomed in the sixties, several things happened. The locations became more exotic, and the hardware more elaborate, at stages threatening to reduce Bond to a special effect. *Thunderball* is an excellent example of this. Its plot concerns the theft of two nuclear bombs which threaten the future of the world. Connery's Bond continues to be an elegant, unruffled ironist in a world of sensation but, when he makes a spectacular airborne escape over the rooftops early on in the film, one can see that the movie is becoming rather more interested in the gadgetry than in nuances of character.

Spies galore
The Bond series was so successful that it produced a massive spin-off of spy and secret agent films – in Britain, *The Ipcress File* (1965) with Michael Caine as Harry Palmer, in America *Our Man Flint* (1965) and *The Silencers* (1966). There were also the anti-Bond movies like Joseph Losey's savagely satirical *Modesty Blaise* (1966), and Martin Ritt's grim adaptation of John Le Carré's novel, *The Spy Who Came in from the Cold* (1966), where the seediness of the secret service is laid bare.

The formula, though, proved to be almost invincible. Audiences have flocked to the Bond movies as sure-fire guarantees of tension and titillation, and of an atmosphere

For once what the publicity posters promised and the films delivered were one and the same. James Bond's effect on the world's most beautiful women and evil villains, and the cool ironic manner with which he handled both, made him an instant box-office hit. Though the series of Bond films increasingly began to concentrate on gadgets at the expense of character, each film has virtually been guaranteed a place among the top box-office hits in its year of release.

that somehow combines the morality of a boy's comic with the upmarket lewdness of *Playboy*. There have only been two real threats to the continuity of Bond's popularity – one slight, one major.

The minor was the growth of the feminist movement, and the objections to Bond's predatory nature and to the sexual violence of some of the advertising. The impact of such criticism seems to have been comfortably absorbed. However, the major hiccups occured when Connery, the chief asset of the series (along with Ken Adam's sets), thought he had tired of the role. His first replacement, George Lazenby, was unsuitable, and the movie, *On Her Majesty's Secret Service* (1969), was the series' only comparative failure. But then Roger Moore successfully stepped in, and the problem was solved – for another decade, at least. And Connery has found that it is never wise to say "never" to Bond.

The casting of Moore showed how flexible the formula was. It is simply a matter of updating the technology and themes, and making adjustments to the hero to suit him to the specific period. Little by little, the classless rebel of the sixties has become the podgy gentleman patriot of the eighties. From Kennedy's favorite reading, James Bond has become, according to President Reagan, "a hero to inspire our times". In time, he has become all things to all men, though remaining only one thing to some women.

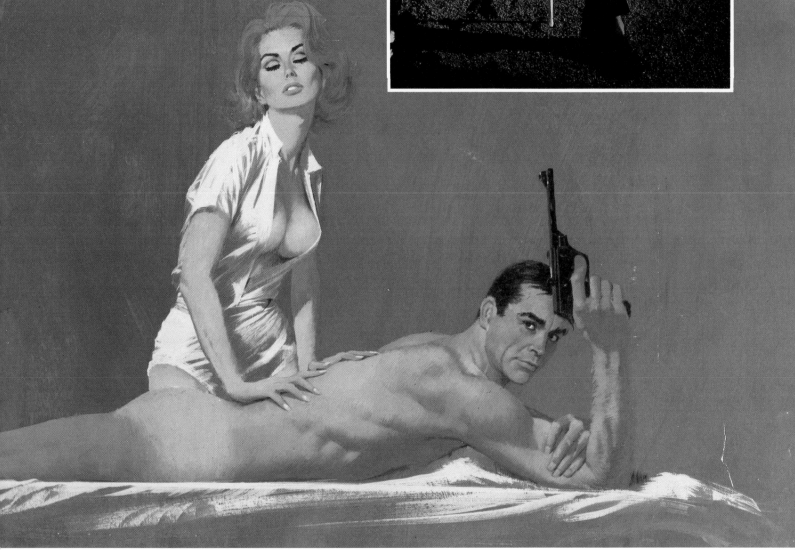

War

THE DIRTY DOZEN (MKH-MGM 1967)
Director: Robert Aldrich

It is quite an achievement to make one of the most popular of all American war films at a time of America's most unpopular war. One of the reasons for the success of *The Dirty Dozen* is probably the ambivalence of director Robert Aldrich to the subject matter and the script. The result is a divided film which managed to appeal to hawks and doves alike.

The formula is a traditional one, from war films such as *The Guns of Navarone*: the dangerous mission undertaken by a group of hand-picked men. The mission this time is to kill some German officers who are stationed at a French castle. The twist is provided by the selection of the men – an expendable group of psychopaths, murderers and sexual obsessives who are given the suicidal job as an alternative to prison and execution. The first part of the film is to show the transformation of a bunch of social misfits into a crack commando unit. The last part deals with the mission itself.

According to Aldrich, there had been four or five aborted scripts before he had come onto the project, and the script he inherited from Nunnally Johnson was more suitable for

war movies of an earlier time. He brought in the writer Lukas Heller, who succeeded in transforming a 1947 picture into a 1967 picture. "Most people were fascinated by the anarchy of the picture's first two-thirds," says Aldrich, "and tolerated and were excited and/or stimulated and/or entertained by the last third."

Sweeping heroics

The first part of the film is strongly anti-authoritarian and in some ways, as the critic Andrew Sarris says, "a glorification of the drop-out". Younger audiences might well have responded to the initial, gleeful iconoclasm of the movie and its unusual morality. Later it is hard to avoid being swept along by the heroics. Aldrich has insisted that he wanted to show that Americans did hideous things as well as the Germans during war time. When the Jim Brown character drops hand grenades in the ventilation systems that are already saturated with gasoline, causing German soldiers to be burned alive, Aldrich said that he intended we should compare that action with some of the atrocities committed in the name of America in Vietnam.

However, it is doubtful whether many in the audience were making such fine moral distinctions at that stage of the film. It knows who the heroes and villains are and is caught up in the excitement.

Basically, the film succeeds as a thrilling war film in a familiar tradition: by the end, its anarchy and ambivalence have been diluted. Contributing to the success is not only Aldrich's characteristically muscular and energizing direction, but the vivid performances of an exceptionally well-chosen cast. The originality is in the casting of heavies as the heroes: Lee Marvin, all taciturn toughness as the commanding officer; John Cassavetes (an Oscar nominee) as the most colorful of the psychopaths; Charles Bronson, Telly Savalas, and Donald Sutherland (chosen, according to Sutherland, because of the size of his ears) all making a big impression before they had fully exploded into superstardom.

Ambivalent meaning

For some, *The Dirty Dozen* is an anti-war movie in that it shows war as an arena fit only for madmen and psychopaths. For others, the majority perhaps, it is a vivid yarn, whose rude characterization and explicit violence serve to give an additional flavor of realism. "I do think that war brings out both the best and worst in men," says Aldrich. The critics attacked him for glorifying violence, but maybe the very moral ambiguity of the film chimed in with the feelings of a confused time. It was to presage the savage satire of Robert Altman's war comedy *M*A*S*H* (1970) and the complex megalomaniac morality of the hero of Franklin J. Schaffner's *Patton* (1970). Aldrich's percentage from the exceptional box-office takings enabled him to buy his own film studio, from where he was to make incomparably more subtle and sophisticated films that were to be incomparably less successful.

Above: *Donald Sutherland was such a success that he was soon selected to star in* **M★A★S★H** *(1970) and* **Klute** *(1971).*

Top Left: *Inside the Nazi-held chateau, Lee Marvin and Charles Bronson struggle out of their German uniforms used for disguise.*

Left: *A preliminary muster of the Dozen reveals some of Hollywood's biggest and toughest heavies including Lee Marvin in charge and Telly Savalas.*

Gangster
BONNIE AND CLYDE (Tatira-Hiller/WB 1967)
Director: Arthur Penn

"I wanted the ballad quality of the thing," said director Arthur Penn, explaining his use of color for *Bonnie and Clyde*, a thirties-style gangster project which in the past had usually been shot in black-and-white. "And I thought the more we used color, the more we were telling the story as recalled as a legend, rather than the actual events. We went to no pains at all to recreate terribly realistically the details and textures of the times." This is also reflected in the choice of the handsome Warren Beatty and the stunning Faye Dunaway to play the unattractive Clyde Barrow and Bonnie Parker, who had a short, tragic career in crime during the Depression.

The film was a colossal success. The reason for this is that, despite being a period piece, the film spoke to the times. There is even something about its rhythm – its wild leaps between comedy and violence – that is quite unlike the gangster movie's usual terse, documentary style, and seems to catch the nervous energy of a youthful, confused, freewheeling age. But the movie's modernity runs much deeper than that.

Rebels on the road
Bonnie and Clyde are presented as social drop-outs, alienated from a society that is seen as devitalized and decayed. Clyde's brother Buck (Gene Hackman), Buck's wife Blanche (Estelle Parsons) and a driver, C. W. Moss (Michael J. Pollard), join them in their exploits. The gang takes to the road and lives out of the car in a way that many disaffected young people of the sixties would recognize as analogous to their own formless lives. Bonnie and Clyde are presented as the hippies of an earlier generation, humiliating the established order, having fun, and generally acting out a vaguely directed programme of social revolt that accords with a sixties feeling of youthful protest, particularly against the Vietnam war.

Feeding the film's fame was unquestionably the controversy it provoked. *Bonnie and Clyde* was accused of social irresponsibility, of romanticizing criminals and of encouraging violence (given the painfulness of the violence in the film, this latter charge is quite extraordinary). The gangster film has always been potentially the most subversive of film genres, because of its tendency to make heroes out of criminals and of its criticism of prevailing social conditions. *Bonnie and Clyde* was subjected to some of the most savage arguments since Hawks's *Scarface* (1932). Critics were split down the middle. Indeed, in one famous incident, the critic of *Time* magazine, Joseph Morgenstern, savaged the movie one week as "a squalid shoot-out for the moron trade", and then, in the following week's column, took it all back and talked of the movie's "dazzling artistry".

Most critics had to concede the extraordinary accomplishment of the film – its splendid performances, Burnett Guffey's stunning photography, David Newman and Robert Benton's razor-sharp dialogue and Arthur Penn's percussive and dynamic direction. Still, many fine films have not had the success of *Bonnie and Clyde*. It was not the movie's quality that made it such a big hit but its notoriety – rather like the Barrow gang, in fact.

Blood red
Two other factors towards its success should be mentioned: namely, its sex and violence. The film has a controversial sexual motif. Clyde's impotence contributes to his sense of inferiority and it is implied that his criminal activities were partly attempts at self-assertion. Also the violence of the film is genuinely disturbing, for three main reasons. The film is structured in such a way that we are encouraged to identify with the Barrow gang before the extreme violence gets underway, so that when it comes, it is especially painful, as if we cannot avoid the bullets any more than the victims. The color highlights the amount of blood spilt: no gangster film before *Bonnie and Clyde* had so much red in it. Finally, the violence seemed both a contemplation and a prophecy of a mood of savage frustration that was slowly sweeping the country. In the slow-motion ballet of brutality that concludes the film when Bonnie and Clyde are shot to pieces by Frank Hamer's posse, Penn has said that the feeling he had in his mind and wanted to convey was something like the shock of the John Kennedy assassination: the moment when the hopes of a whole generation seemed suddenly paralyzed. The horrific detail when part of Clyde's head is blown off in the shooting is an anguished allusion to the Kennedy murder.

This final scene has another purpose. The massive over-reaction by a vengeful establishment seems to anticipate the convulsive violence to come in the backlash against permissiveness that will tear America apart in 1968. *Bonnie and Clyde* was truly an explosive movie experience. It became vital material for discussion not only for cineastes, but for sociologists, politicians, the moral reformers, and the committed and caring younger generation to whom it spoke in a powerful, urgent, despairing tone of voice.

Top left: *Bonnie (Faye Dunaway) and Clyde (Warren Beatty) are self-publicists who enjoy posing for photographers. Bonnie also writes doggerel verse for the newspapers!*

Above: *So they think they've got problems because he's impotent? In the original script Clyde was gay, Bonnie a nympho and both were making it with driver C.W. Moss!*

Right: *For the film's final and all too inevitable ambush scene, Faye Dunaway's leg was tied to the car's emergency brake enabling her to lean right over and die at a dreadful angle.*

Comedy
THE GRADUATE (Turman/Embassy 1967)
Director: Mike Nichols

With *Bonnie and Clyde* and *The Graduate*, Hollywood suddenly struck gold with an effective appeal to the youth market, the eighteen to twenty-five age group who were increasingly beginning to dominate the film audience. Ben (Dustin Hoffman) in *The Graduate* caught the imagination of young film audiences in the way that the hero of J. D. Salinger's novel *The Catcher in the Rye* (1954) had seemed to embody the confusions and yearnings of a whole adolescent generation a decade earlier. Numerous critics pointed to this comparison between the two works, partly to suggest that Ben in *The Graduate* seems more a rather old-fashioned fifties youth than a typical sixties one: his character is apolitical, passive and virginal rather than virile and committed. But the film's success might well have had something to do with the way it blends its modern sheen with concealed traditional pleasures. Its pleasure and popularity were enhanced by the bitter-sweet songs of Simon and Garfunkel that accompany the narrative.

The action is mainly seen through the eyes of Ben, a confused twenty-one-year-old who is worried about the future but who does not simply want to follow the commercial path of his affluent family and their friends. His life becomes complicated when he is embroiled in an affair with an older woman, Mrs Robinson (Anne Bancroft). It becomes impossible when he falls in love with Mrs Robinson's daughter, Elaine (Katharine Ross).

Sexual victim
Director Mike Nichols gets a lot of saucy humor out of the risqué affair, particularly through the exploitation of Ben's naivety. He is sexually inexperienced, cannot handle an assignation, and his notion of sexual arousal is to put his hand tentatively on Mrs Robinson's breast as if he were feeling her pulse. The curious formality of the relationship, and the poise of the performances, gave the coupling a kind of impudence and surprise that had tickled audiences in earlier sex comedies of the decade like Tony Richardson's *Tom Jones* and Billy Wilder's *Irma La Douce*. Nevertheless, the relationship also shows Ben as a victim of a predatory adult, which is a theme pursued through the film – innocent youth exploited and betrayed by a corrupt, decadent and discredited older generation. This was to become a clarion call for the times.

The Graduate uses a traditional structure which had proved its popularity in the past. Its rite-of-passage form – the growth from youth to experience, particularly sexual experience – is to be followed in *Goodbye Columbus* (1969) and coarsened in later, highly successful college comedies like *Porky's* (1982). Ben is also a kind of campus Oedipus, in love with both mother and daughter. It is not surprising that, in his first meeting with Elaine, he behaves rather as Hamlet does towards Ophelia – the pain and disgust inside himself producing a desire to hurt anyone who comes near him.

As well as a comic movie and a film about the growing pains of youth, *The Graduate* is also very romantic, a good example of how popular cinema can rework an old formula for a new age and make it accessible to younger audiences

Right: *Benjamin Braddock (Dustin Hoffman) wants to talk about art, or anything. Mrs Robinson (Anne Bancroft), who majored in fine arts, just wants sex – or so she thinks... until Ben falls in love with her daughter, Elaine.*

Bottom inset: *Undeterred by the fact that Elaine (Katharine Ross) has just married a man she does not love, Ben fights off the wedding party with a cross, uses it to jam the church door and together with Elaine escapes into a happier future on a passing bus.*

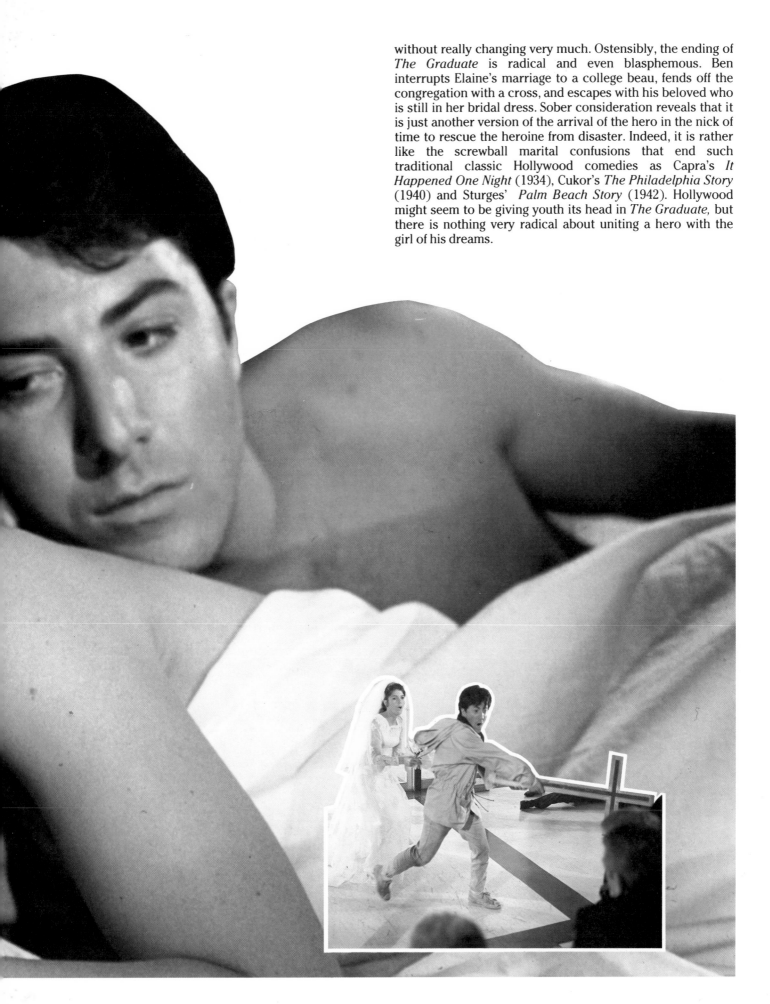

without really changing very much. Ostensibly, the ending of *The Graduate* is radical and even blasphemous. Ben interrupts Elaine's marriage to a college beau, fends off the congregation with a cross, and escapes with his beloved who is still in her bridal dress. Sober consideration reveals that it is just another version of the arrival of the hero in the nick of time to rescue the heroine from disaster. Indeed, it is rather like the screwball marital confusions that end such traditional classic Hollywood comedies as Capra's *It Happened One Night* (1934), Cukor's *The Philadelphia Story* (1940) and Sturges' *Palm Beach Story* (1942). Hollywood might seem to be giving youth its head in *The Graduate,* but there is nothing very radical about uniting a hero with the girl of his dreams.

133

Science Fiction
2001: A SPACE ODYSSEY (MGM 1968)
Director: Stanley Kubrick

Although collaborators like writer Arthur C. Clarke and effects specialists Wally Veevers and Douglas Trumbull were important to the success of *2001*, the film is basically a triumph for its producer-director, Stanley Kubrick. No cinema epic since D. W. Griffith's *Intolerance* (1916) had been so completely the vision of one man. What is more remarkable about the film's success is that it has no stars (the filmic variety, anyway) and very little plot.

At that time, of course, audiences were less familiar with the hardware and spectacle of space travel than they are today. It was released before the Apollo mission beamed back the first authentic television images from the moon. Kubrick's remarkable attempt to create an authentic otherworldly experience had the appeal of novelty. It seemed peculiarly a film of its time. Space travel could be responded to by young audiences as the ultimate psychedelic "trip". Also the relative sparsity of dialogue allowed audiences to respond to the film as a visual and musical experience, perhaps anticipating the demands of future audiences for visual stimuli rather than verbal sophistication and wit.

2001 set a fashion for elaborate special effects in science-fiction films, sometimes at the expense of plot and characterization, that became dominant in the seventies. It was filmed in Super Panavision (by Geoffrey Unsworth) and presented originally in single-screen Cinerama. Special effects were by Wally Veevers, Douglas Trumbull, Con Pederson and Tom Howard.

Mysterious monolith

But *2001* is also a cerebral film of ideas, and a lot of younger college audiences went again and again to tease out some of the themes. The film debates the relationship between Man and Technology. An astonishing match-cut between the swirling bone of a primeval ape and a floating spacecraft of the twenty-first century seems implicitly to question how far man has developed from his primitive origins. The story is divided into three movements: "The Dawn of Man"; "Mission to Jupiter"; and "Beyond the Infinite". All three parts are linked by the appearance at various stages of a mysterious rectangular monolith that seems to symbolize the next stage of knowledge, towards which man is always aspiring. The film is about man's constant quest after new intelligence, as he takes what Kubrick describes as the "next step of his evolutionary destiny".

The music in *2001* is especially important. Richard Strauss's tone poem, "Thus Spake Zarathustra", expresses the immensity of man's potential; Johann Strauss's "Blue Danube" waltz accompanies the spacecraft in a wholly ingenious concept of the music of the spheres. The film's most sympathetic character is the computer HAL, and a number of questions are raised when HAL has a nervous breakdown and takes revenge on his creators. Man might have created this technology, but can he control it? *2001* demonstrates that Stanley Kubrick can certainly control his.

"If the film stirs the emotions and penetrates the subconscious of the viewer," said Kubrick, "if it stimulates, however inchoately, his mythological and religious yearnings and impulses, then it has succeeded." *2001* did all of these things. It was an enormous hit because it was a visual adventure on a scale that had scarcely been seen on a screen before. It was also an intellectual enquiry for a young audience that was more critical and questioning about the world then than it seems to be today, and who responded to the film's irony, intelligence and scepticism. Its success anticipated two important seventies trends: the director as superstar; and the explosion of interest in films of fantasy and science fiction.

BUTCH CASSIDY AND THE SUNDANCE KID (Campanile/Fox 1969)

Director: George Roy Hill

"I gave you *Shane*, and you gave me *Gunga Din!*" This was screenwriter William Goldman's response to George Roy Hill's direction of his script for *Butch Cassidy and the Sundance Kid*. "What we really got," said Hill, "was the Laurel and Hardy of Deadwood Gulch."

It hardly needs saying that the star and sex appeal of Paul Newman and Robert Redford contributed enormously to this movie's box-office bonanza. Nevertheless, the way their roles were conceived was equally important to the occasion. Newman and Redford appear as the most friendly, likeable pair of outlaws seen in a western. Their knockabout, adventuresome relationship recalls the mischief of Huckleberry Finn and Tom Sawyer and the wisecracking slapstick of Hope and Crosby, Martin and Lewis.

In exploiting the element of laughter and joyfulness in comradeship, the movie revived a tradition which had fallen somewhat into abeyance during the fifties when moody Method actors like Brando, James Dean or Montgomery Clift had established a new kind of aloof and withdrawn movie hero who occupied a position of self-imposed romantic isolation.

Outlaws out of touch

The central theme of *Butch Cassidy and the Sundance Kid* is the same as that of a number of key westerns of the sixties, notably John Ford's *The Man Who Shot Liberty Valance* and Sam Peckinpah's *The Wild Bunch* – the dying of the old West and the reduction of the cowboy to an anachronism. At the beginning of the film, Butch is dismayed to find a new automated bank which will be much more difficult to rob ("What happened to the old bank? It was beautiful!"). Throughout the film they are relentlessly pursued by a posse, which is scarcely seen but which seems unshakeable and

sophisticated in its tracking methods. This posse symbolizes progress and the modern world, which will overtake Butch and Sundance sooner or later and signal their death.

Butch and Sundance has a lot in common with *The Wild Bunch* – a daring train raid, slow-motion deaths, and a violent last stand when time has run out. But it is possible that the differences are even more significant. The humor of this movie and its likeable leads have already been mentioned. In some ways, the tone is more important than the theme. The movie seems cool and modern, rather than stately and serious as in the classic western. Burt Bacharach provides a bouncy pop score, whose hit song "Rain Drops Keep Fallin' on My Head" provides a light comic interlude in the film (indeed, almost the equivalent of a promo pop video of today). The photographic style is self-conscious and richly textured, in sequences such as the journey to Bolivia using

important. Butch and Sundance may bicker over whether to jump off a cliff and they may be in love with the same girl, Mattie (Katharine Ross), but they never contemplate parting. Like Truffaut's *Jules and Jim* (1961), *Butch and Sundance* is a celebration of an ideal friendship between men, which is made to seem the most natural thing in the world. The theme has a long tradition in American culture, and *Butch and Sundance* did it so well that everyone wanted to get in on the act. The proliferation of "buddy movies" was to be one of the features of American cinema early in the coming decade.

handsomely mounted stills worthy of inclusion in a color supplement magazine. In an era when style counted for a great deal, *Butch and Sundance* had style in abundance.

Just good friends

The genial anarchy of the two outlaws undoubtedly clicked with younger audiences: indeed, Paul Newman has always used the western to indulge his wilder, more iconoclastic spirit. As in *Bonnie and Clyde* and *Easy Rider*, sympathetic outsiders were part of the filmic flavor of the time. The high jinks are to end in death, of course, but unlike the purgative blood-letting that concludes *The Wild Bunch*, this movie handles the finale with wit and affection, skilfully freezing the frame at the precise point before the carnage gets too painful.

It is the interplay between the two main characters that is

Youth Protest
EASY RIDER (Raybert-Pando/Columbia 1969)
Director: Dennis Hopper

"Two pictures nearly destroyed the industry," said Ned Tannen, when president of Universal Pictures. "One was *The Sound of Music*, which was such a huge hit that all the studios tried to copy it, investing in big-budget films, mainly musicals, that were all commercial disasters. The other was *Easy Rider*, which spawned a series of low-budget youth movies that were so bad, most were never released."

Easy Rider had taken everybody by surprise. Produced by Peter Fonda and directed by Dennis Hopper (a new venture for both these young actors), the film cost $400,000 to make and took about twenty-five times that amount at the box-office. "It isn't hard to make a successful movie," said Hopper at the time (he has not made a successful movie since). "Just feed the elements into your computer and the answers will come out." The elements in this case were correctly diagnosed and very skilfully mixed.

Road movie
First of all, the heroes seem representative of the time – rootless rebels whose alienation from contemporary society and whose romantic gestures of freedom take the form of a pilgrimage across America on the proceeds of their heroin sales. Their motorbikes become emblems of both their rebelliousness (as in Brando's 1954 movie *The Wild One*) and their independence and mobility (Robert Pilsig was to philosophize on that kind of life-style in his trendy tome, *Zen and the Art of Motorcycle Maintenance*). The cross-country bike scenes are accompanied by evocative rock music of the period from performers like Steppenwolf, the Byrds and Jimi Hendrix which further emphasize the identification between the movie and the rebellious young.

At the time, the film felt fresh and modern. It popularized the look of a psychedelic experience. Its structure had the seeming casualness of cult writers like Ken Kesey and Tom Wolfe, feeling improvisational more than finished, a happening more than a narrative, journalism more than art. In fact, this is something of an illusion, since the film is technically accomplished (finely photographed by Laszlo Kovacs and edited by Henry Jaglom) and has a coherence of tone and motif – a series of bids for freedom checked by sudden eruptions of violence – that gives it tension and a sense of ominousness.

It also had a sense of character. In particular, Jack Nicholson's performance as the alcoholic Southern lawyer, George Hanson – a middle-aged parasite who attaches himself to Billy and Wyatt in a last desperate fling at youth and freedom – is a splendid achievement, winning him the first of numerous Oscar nominations. George is the heart of the film and, at one stage, expresses its theme. "This used to be a helluva country. I can't tell you what's wrong," he says. "They're scared not of you but of what you represent to them: freedom."

Anarchic symbols
The shocking violence of the film's ending – when Billy and Wyatt are shot by bigoted rednecks – was attacked by some as being unprepared and excessively pessimistic. Yet it seems the inevitable culmination of the antagonism between youth and age in the movie, which would explode into brutal confrontation (as did the protests against the Vietnam war). Billy and Wyatt are revealing sixties youth symbols in the sense that they are not protecting society against its enemies: society itself is seen as the enemy.

The rebellious hippie generation certainly agreed. It is surely not accidental that three of the most popular films of the late sixties – *Bonnie and Clyde*, *Easy Rider* and *Butch Cassidy and the Sundance Kid* – end in exactly the same way – in the shooting down of their two anarchic central characters. The tone is slightly different: angry and poetic *(Bonnie and Clyde)*; abrupt and sickening *(Easy Rider)*; inevitable and elegiac *(Butch and Sundance)*. These endings reflect the violence of the age, but they also represent the death of a mood of anarchic protest and youthful rebellion as a backlash of social retaliation sets in. Thematically, *Easy Rider* is an eloquent elegy for the sixties. Logistically, it is powerfully prophetic of seventies Hollywood, when suddenly the old guard were to be swept aside by a bright new generation of movie brats.

Left: *"We blew it." After a bad time with hookers and drugs in New Orleans, they set off for Florida. But a truck-driver accidentally shoots Billy and then comes back deliberately to kill Wyatt.*

Below: *"I Wonder Where My Easy Rider's Gone", sang Mae West in* **She Done Him Wrong** *(1933). Gone to find America, Billy (Dennis Hopper – left) and Wyatt "Captain America" (Peter Fonda) pick up an alcoholic lawyer, George Hanson (Jack Nicholson), in Texas on their way to New Orleans. But he is murdered before they get there.*

CHAPTER FIVE:

THE SEVENTIES

The film companies made a gradual but sustained recovery from the large losses and weak film attendance of the early seventies. This marked an apparent turning point for the industry as a whole and the end of that virtually continuous decline experienced during the post-war period.

The big success story of the decade was the work of a small group of new young film-makers, some of whom seemed to conquer Hollywood straight after graduating from UCLA. The young director William Friedkin had two of the biggest hits of the early seventies, *The French Connection* (1971) and *The Exorcist* (1973). The former was an example of a cycle of movies about "rogue cops" – another huge success was the Clint Eastwood film *Dirty Harry* (1971), directed by Don Siegel. These reflected many contemporary anxieties about the violence of urban life. *The Exorcist* was the most successful of another phenomenon of the seventies, the American horror film, which took cinema violence to new extremes and where attitudes ranged all the way from murderous misogyny to anarchic apocalypse.

However, the big hit of the early seventies was Francis Ford Coppola's majestic gangster movie, *The Godfather* (1972), which established Coppola as one of the major directors of the decade. In their intuitions about power, business and secret societies, *The Godfather* and its equally remarkable sequel, *Godfather II* (1974), seemed influenced by a national paranoia induced by the Watergate scandal. At the end of the decade, Coppola made another mighty statement about the Vietnam experience, *Apocalypse Now* (1979).

Right: ***Star Wars'*** *director George Lucas described himself as something of a "toy maker", and here are two of his creations C-3PO and R2-D2 who provided an unusual kind of double act that helped account for the film's staggering success.*

Top right and far right: *Hollywood cleverly manipulating the audience in a more traditional way in* **"10"** *(1979). Newly wed Jenny (Bo Derek) is rated eleven on a one-to-ten scale of beauty by middle-aged song composer George (Dudley Moore). Publicity shots like these helped* **"10"** *to notch up $37m in US rentals alone.*

Setting an example

Coppola had graduated from film school in the sixties and established his credentials within the industry at a remarkably young age. He became a kind of godfather figure and inspiration to other aspirant young directors who wished to emulate his success. Two of them not only emulated it: they surpassed it. With *Jaws* (1975), Steven Spielberg attracted a mass audience of a size that had not been seen since *The Sound of Music*. Even this remarkable achievement, however, was topped by George Lucas' *Star Wars* (1977) which, in an amazingly short time, became the second biggest money-making movie ever, after *Gone with the Wind*.

A number of new trends were evident during the seventies. The new generation of producer-writer-directors were making films aimed at the younger audiences. The hit films were rarely conceived as a vehicle for one or more leading stars, as had so often been the case in the past. *The Sting* (1973) with the Newman-Redford duo, and the Streisand-Redford co-starrer, *The Way We Were* (1973), were exceptions, but few of the record-breaking hits of the decade – *Star Wars, Jaws, Close Encounters of the Third Kind* (1977), *The Exorcist, Alien* (1979) – relied for their success on star names.

Except for the dependably monolithic Clint Eastwood (and even he had his experimental moments), the new generation of crowd-pullers, like Jack Nicholson, Al Pacino, Robert De Niro and Dustin Hoffman, were more "character actors" than stars. They moulded their screen personas to fit a wide range of roles. Also, in the highly popular science-fiction and disaster movies, the actors were often dwarfed by the striking and elaborate special effects.

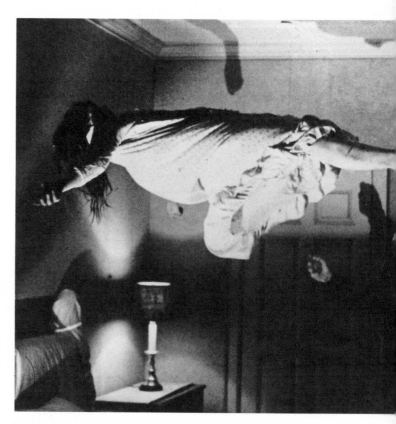

Above: *Two Jesuit priests (Max Von Sydow, Jason Miller) try to drive out the evil spirit from a levitating child (Linda Blair) in **The Exorcist** (1973).* **Right:** *Publicity artwork for **Jaws** (1975), a monster success at the box-office.*

Below: *Luke Skywalker (Mark Hamill) rides again in **The Empire Strikes Back** (1980).*

Breaking with tradition

If the Vietnam and post-Watergate era in the United States initiated an enquiring scepticism on the part of younger film-makers, this could be seen most clearly in the new attitudes to traditional subjects. The most popular war film of the decade, for example, was Robert Altman's irreverent *M*A*S*H* (1970), set during the Korean War but, to all intents and purposes, Sergeant Bilko in Vietnam. The film's success gave Altman's career an enormous fillip and allowed him the freedom to develop some of the most offbeat and innovative mainstream films of the decade, notably his country-music epic *Nashville* (1975).

Right: *Capt Willard (Martin Sheen) in* **Apocalypse Now** *(1979).*
Far right: *Popeye Doyle (Gene Hackman) meets Barthelemy (Bernard Fresson, right) in* **French Connection II** *(1975).*

Above: *Time off from the army hospital in Korea for the weary doctors of* **M★A★S★H** *(1970).* **Left:** *Sgt Mike Vronsky (Robert De Niro) in* **The Deer Hunter** *(1978).*

Similarly, during a crisis of confidence in the national psyche, one would not expect the most noble and affirmative of American genres, the western, to continue along traditional lines. Significantly, the most popular western of the seventies was Mel Brooks' madcap comedy *Blazing Saddles* (1973), which brought a wind of change to traditional scenes such as the cowboys' meal around the campfire. Cheerful vulgarity was to be a feature of some of the most popular comedies of the decade, as demonstrated by *Smokey and the Bandit* (1977), and *National Lampoon's Animal House* (1978). At the same time, stylish screen comedy did not die. Woody Allen's popularity soared to new heights with *Annie Hall* (1977) and *Manhattan* (1979). Blake Edwards revived the delightful *Pink Panther* series with spectacular success, and had his biggest box-office returns for years with his suave comedy about the menopausal male, *"10"* (1979).

The seventies saw the decline of the two companies most

Right: *Marlon Brando in the role Orson Welles would have given an arm to play, Don Vito Corleone in **The Godfather** (1972).*

clearly identified with traditional family entertainment at the movies, MGM and Disney. The Disney organization became more involved in its various non-film activities such as Disneyland and Disney World, while MGM devoted its new investment to the hotel and casino business. Both companies continued to pursue a highly profitable policy of re-releasing their old pictures. On the other hand, Universal Pictures – for many years the "also ran" among the major companies – made a dramatic comeback. The success of *Airport* (1970), which even one of its stars, Burt Lancaster, had dismissed as "a heap of junk", was followed by winners like *The Sting* and *Jaws*. The fortunes of United Artists were more variable. It won three Best Picture Oscars in consecutive years – Milos Forman's *One Flew Over the Cuckoo's Nest* (1975), John G. Avildsen's *Rocky* (1976) and Woody Allen's *Annie Hall* – but it shared only to a limited extent in the 1979 boom and was ill-prepared for the debâcle of Michael Cimino's doomed western epic, *Heaven's Gate* (1981).

Box-office bungles

Cimino had been given his head on *Heaven's Gate* after the enormous success of his Vietnam film, *The Deer Hunter* (1978). But, by the end of the decade, there were signs that the superstar directors of the new generation were as fallible as everything else in the movie business when it came to guaranteeing sure-fire box-office rewards. Robert Altman had not had a money-maker since *M*A*S*H*. Stanley Kubrick's intensely personal, ravishingly beautiful, historical film *Barry Lyndon* (1975) had failed to achieve the commercial cult classic status of his previous movies, *2001* and *A Clockwork Orange* (1971). Coppola had just about brought in *Apocalypse Now* successfully, but he had almost driven himself and

Below: *Robert Redford and Barbra Streisand in* **The Way We Were** *(1973).*

his financiers mad in the process. After the runaway success of his Gothic horror movie, *Carrie* (1975), Brian De Palma's commercial instincts had faltered, as had those of comedy director Michael Ritchie after the enormous popularity of the delightful *Bad News Bears* (1976). Spielberg had bungled his spectacular comedy, *1941* (1979); *Animal House* director John Landis fumbled his follow-up picture, *The Blues Brothers* (1980).

Of course, a number of these directors were to come storming back in the following decade. But it simply showed that backing successful directors was no more reliable a guide to the box-office than all the other methods financiers had tried. It has hard to keep pace with a decade that had started with the saccharine sentiment "Love means never having to say you're sorry ..." *(Love Story)* and ended with the suspenseful slogan "In space no one can hear you scream..." *(Alien).* It was impossible to predict the popular musicals when *Sergeant Pepper's Lonely Hearts Club Band* (1978) and *The Wiz* (1978) failed as mysteriously and spectacularly as *Saturday Night Fever* (1977) and *Grease* (1978) succeeded. Who could have foretold that the events of the nuclear drama *The China Syndrome* (1979) would have been repeated at Three Mile Island within days of the film's release, giving an enormous surge to the movie's topicality and popularity? Billy Wilder probably had the right idea when he said that the only safe thing in the movie industry is to say "No" to everything: nine times out of ten, you will be proved right.

But what if the tenth is *Star Wars*? ...

Top left: *It's not a game of chance the way Paul Newman plays in* **The Sting** *(1973).* **Above:** *Alien (1979) starred Sigourney Weaver.* **Below:** *Red Buttons, Shelley Winters and Jack Albertson in* **The Poseidon Adventure** *(1972).*

The biggest hits
The Top Ten box-office movies of the seventies were, in order: *Star Wars* (1977); *Jaws* (1975); *The Godfather* (1972); *Grease* (1978); *Superman* (1979); *Close Encounters of the Third Kind* (1977); *Saturday Night Fever* (1977); *The Sting* (1973); *The Exorcist* (1973); *National Lampoon's Animal House* (1978).

The biggest stars
The Top Ten box-office stars between 1970 and 1979 were, in order: Clint Eastwood; Burt Reynolds; Barbra Streisand; Robert Redford; Paul Newman; Steve McQueen; John Wayne; Woody Allen; Dustin Hoffman; Al Pacino.

All-time favorite stars
The Top Ten box-office stars from 1932 to 1980 were, in order: John Wayne; Gary Cooper; Bing Crosby; Clark Gable; Clint Eastwood; Bob Hope; Paul Newman; Doris Day; Rock Hudson; Cary Grant.

Romance
LOVE STORY (Paramount 1970)
Director: Arthur Hiller

In some quarters, *Love Story* has been dismissed as one of the most synthetic and cynical examples of popular film success, playing upon an audience's emotions in the most calculated way. Yet, if its success were as glib and as easy as some have made out, one would have expected a rather different background to the production of the film, which was extremely tortured and tortuous. *Love Story* was a vindication of the faith of one man, studio executive Robert Evans.

Erich Segal's screenplay for *Love Story* had been turned down by six major studios before Evans snapped it up for Paramount in 1969, mainly because he saw a great part in it for his wife at that time, Ali MacGraw. He put Segal to work on writing up the script as a novel, while he set about assembling the film. The star, Ryan O'Neal, was actually the sixth actor to have been offered the role: it had been turned down by Beau Bridges, Jon Voight, Michael Sarrazin, Michael York and Michael Douglas. The film started shooting in January 1970 but two directors (Larry Peerce and Anthony Harvey) left before it was taken over by Arthur Hiller. Segal had completed the novel, but the publisher was so unimpressed that he was only going to open with a run of six thousand copies. Evans persuaded him to make it twenty-five thousand on the agreement that Evans himself would put up a considerable sum for publicity. It was published on St Valentine's Day, and by the time the film was ready for release in December, the book was the number one best seller in both hard and paperback in America. On Evans' part, the whole operation was a masterpiece of pre-selling.

Romeo and Juliet

Leslie Halliwell has summarized the plot of *Love Story* as follows: "Two students marry: she dies." True enough, but there is a bit more to it than that. The writer was an extremely erudite man (a Yale professor of classics) who clearly knew what he was doing. *Love Story* is a kind of modern variation on two very potent myths. The first derives from an observation of Edgar Allan Poe: "the death of a beautiful young woman is the most poetic of subjects." The second derives from Shakespeare. The two lovers in *Love Story* are first divided from each other by class – he is the son of a wealthy banker, she the daughter of an ordinary Italian immigrant – which results in parental opposition to their marriage. They are subsequently to be divided by death. What we have is a modern *Romeo and Juliet*.

In spotting this, Evans revealed his keen filmic and business acumen. One of the surprise hits of the late sixties had been Franco Zeffirelli's film of *Romeo and Juliet* (1968), which is the most popular Shakespearean film ever made. Either consciously or subconsciously, Evans seems to have used Zeffirelli's film as a kind of model. In a world of violence and social change, *Love Story* blandly presents two students who are completely unpoliticized and committed only to their love – like Shakespeare's lovers.

The film makes various concessions to modernity, notably in the frank sexual language of the couple. But mostly it is traditional fare that must have come as a refreshing change to some audiences from the violence and aggressive sexual-

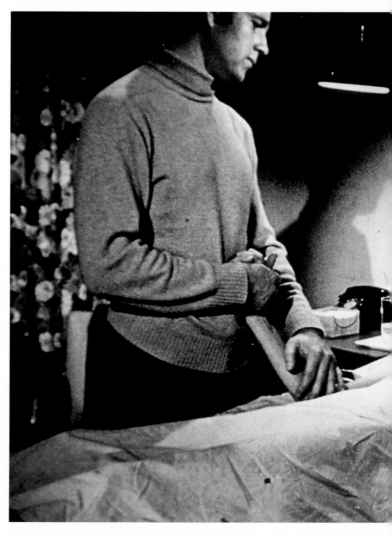

Above and right: *"Love means never having to say you're sorry." No regrets for Jenny (Ali MacGraw) or her husband Oliver (Ryan O'Neal).*

ity of recent cinema. Critics found it morbid. They suggested that it combined the worst elements of a sadistic male fantasy (the hero's fear of confronting a woman on equal terms is relieved by the death of the woman) and a masochistic female fantasy (a tragic ending that is transcended by the bravery of the heroine).

Nevertheless, audiences have often responded to the plight of a romantic heroine who uncomplainingly confronts a noble death: think of Bette Davis in an old Warners' warhorse, *Dark Victory* (1939), or more recently the cancer-racked Debra Winger in *Terms of Endearment* (1983). The performances carry conviction, and the audience of *Love Story* had something they had been denied for a long time: the luxury of a good cry. For the young, it was the courtship film of the day. As Robert Evans put it: "The picture turned out to be a kind of aphrodisiac: wherever it opened, kids would walk out of the theater, arm in arm, in love! It was the 'make-out' picture of the decade." With some variations, *Summer of '42* (1972) repeated the formula with great success, but a sequel, *Oliver's Story* (1978), was seen by audiences as a grotesque betrayal of noble suffering and was a commercial and critical disaster.

Gangster
THE GODFATHER (Alfran/Paramount 1972)
Director: Francis Ford Coppola

After the failure of Martin Ritt's *The Brotherhood* (1968) for Paramount, the studio's worry over *The Godfather* was: would the public come to see a Mafia movie? The executives thought they would and, as part of their new policy, they packed everything into making it the "event" movie of the year (that is, a major production which they would sell as hard as they could and which, according to the president of Paramount Pictures, Frank Yablans, had to contain "emotion, a structured story, jeopardy, romance and action"). On the basis of the first hundred pages of *The Godfather*, Mario Puzo was paid eighty thousand dollars to finish the novel. By the time the film was ready, the novel had sold a million in hardback and twelve million in paperback.

Although the novel's success seemed to guarantee a sizeable movie audience, there was a lot of anxiety during the shooting. Paramount were worried about the casting of Marlon Brando, partly because of his volatile reputation with directors and particularly because he had not had a box-office success for over a decade. The track record of Francis Ford Coppola also gave them pause: he was an obviously talented man, but one who seemed to make intimate arty movies rather than epic melodramas. Added to that were Paramount's apprehensions about setting the film in period (which considerably increased the cost); shooting footage in Sicily rather than in the studio; and the insistence of producer Robert Evans that this three-hour film should play without an interval.

Award-winner
However, the film turned out to be a triumph, both critically and commercially. It won the Best Picture Oscar of 1972 and, with the appearance of *The Godfather, Part II* in 1974, Coppola had made two films which were to resonate across the decade as prime examples of Hollywood's ability to combine intelligent social comment with riveting narrative.

The casting of Brando turned out to be a triumph, too. From his opening scene, where he presides simultaneously over "business" and his daughter's wedding, to his death scene among the orange groves, he exudes a massive patriarchal authority which holds both family and movie together. His performance won him an Oscar. Indeed, the film is exceptionally well cast throughout. It was no surprise that James Caan, Robert Duvall and Al Pacino were also nominated for Oscars. Pacino, as the Don's academic son, Michael, who will succeed his father, comes close to stealing the film altogether: it is a meticulously constructed, awesomely controlled performance.

Blood ties
Many moments in the film have since become famous: the horse's severed head that soaks the bed clothes of a recalcitrant movie producer in blood; the murder in the restaurant, which seals Michael's blood relationship with his Mafia family; in particular, the extraordinary baptism scene near the end when Michael is acting as godfather to his sister's child. At the same time that he is explicitly renouncing Satan and his works, a series of vicious murders

organized by him are being committed to confirm his position as "godfather" in the other sense.

The extreme violence of the film excited and shocked many, provoking a great deal of comment. It was also said that *The Godfather* glamorized gangsters. It is not that simple and the reasons for the success of the film are complex and many-sided. There is no doubt that the film brilliantly combined the most potent elements of two extremely popular genres – gangster film and family melodrama.

Analysis of power
As a gangster film, *The Godfather* invites an audience into an exciting and dangerous world. It also has something of the anarchic energy and social criticism of the characteristic gangster film. For Marlon Brando, *The Godfather* was "a picture of corporate America", whilst Coppola said, "The Mafia is no different from any other big, greedy, profit-making corporation in America" – was he thinking of Hollywood? There is an ambiguity there, of course. On the one hand, the film exposes what it sees as the ruthlessness and violence of capitalist enterprise. On the other, it makes such enterprise seem dynamic and compelling. As the critic David Thomson pointed out, the things in which Don Corleone believes – "peace on the streets, honor in profit and hard work, distaste for narcotics, support of a Christian moral and social ethic, belief in neighborliness, and the schizoid inability to relate wholesome ends and a crook's methods" – are practically indistinguishable from the programme on which President Nixon was re-elected that same year. The film slides tantalizingly back and forth between the proposition that "Big Business is Crime" and "Crime is Big Business".

In the name of the family
As a family drama, *The Godfather* has all the character, identification figures and variety of incident that one associates with the classic soap operas, from *Dallas* to *Heimat*. It is about family planning. The Corleones are less like Capone than like the Borgias. Action is planned around family rituals: meals, weddings, baptisms, funerals. Indeed, Corleone rarely strays outside his own home and part of the force of the movie comes from this sense of influence without movement, the sense of a society being controlled by a man in a dark room of his own (white) house. The transformation of Michael from returning American war hero to cold-blooded killer is triggered by the code of honor which compels him to murder out of family loyalty. "I'm with you now, I'm with you," he says to his wounded father in the hospital, and, from then on, there is a slow and shocking transformation in which the character's face is both literally and metaphorically reconstructed. But part of the movie's power comes through the violence perpetrated in the name of family, in the name of generalized values hardly different from those in *Little Women* – good housekeeping, hard work and respect for one's parents. Interestingly, when Michael and his fiancée Kay (Diane Keaton) go to the movies, they see the heartwarming Catholic family drama, *The Bells of St Mary's* (1945).

The Godfather turned out to be a rich brew of fascinating themes – America, family, business, violence, crime, as well as all the qualities that Yablans had mentioned earlier. It provoked controversy and comment, but united critics and public in popular acclaim. The two *Godfather* movies remain the best gangster films ever made in America. It is hard to see how, in their particular genre, they can ever be bettered.

Right: *Marlon Brando at the wedding of his daughter Connie (Talia Shire) to Rizzi (Gianni Russo – top left). However, Rizzi breaks the family code of honor when he beats his new wife and is in turn attacked by her brother, played by James Caan (**below**). **Bottom right:** The Godfather enjoys the fruits of his labors.*

Comedy
THE STING (Bill-Phillips/Zanuck-Brown/Universal 1973)
Director: George Roy Hill

Ostensibly, *The Sting* subscribes to one of the most durable and dubious of Hollywood's principles: that nothing succeeds like the repetition of success. It is a film quite clearly designed to exploit the popularity of *Butch Cassidy and the Sundance Kid.* It once again teams Paul Newman and Robert Redford as a friendly duo; it is once again directed by George Roy Hill; it again uses period detail for background decoration (here the Chicago of the Depression years); and it again has a self-conscious, anachronistic but highly colorful selection of soundtrack music to leave an audience in a bright frame of mind (the piano rags of Scott Joplin). Because the film has such a high level of performing and technical professionalism, it must have looked to everyone that it could not miss. It didn't. What is more, it pleased the critics as well as audiences, winning the Best Film and Best Directing Oscars of 1973.

The Sting's major pleasures come from three sources: period, plot and performance. It is not simply that the film recreates an era: it does so in a very stylish and stylized way. The characterization – tough gangster, English gentleman, put-upon waitress, moll – is a parade of imitation Damon Runyon. The movie is a self-conscious recreation of a past based less on reality than on books, movies and cultural mythology. It happened to be released in the middle of a nostalgia boom, helped by the tremendous popularity of George Lucas' *American Graffiti* (1973) – a boom which was to end, catastrophically, with *The Great Gatsby* a year later. During a time of crisis, people were looking to the past for comfort and escape. *The Sting* certainly supplied that.

It also supplies quite a deft narrative to go with the nostalgia. The plot concerns the attempt of two conmen (Redford and Newman) to secure revenge on a ruthless gangster (Robert Shaw). As befits a story of deceit and double-cross, the plot's poker-faced elaborations of bluff and double-bluff often catch out an audience as much as the characters. The card game on the train, or the elaborate build-up to the film's denouement, carry a few surprises and shock waves for the unwary.

Buddy movie
In contrast to *Butch Cassidy and the Sundance Kid*, the characters played by Newman and Redford in *The Sting* are relatively uninteresting: indeed, it is doubtful whether many people could remember what the characters are called (all the more credit to Robert Redford, then, for being nominated for an Oscar for his performance). Nevertheless, Newman and Redford are essential to the film's success. In fact, it is hard to imagine the film working without them. They flesh out the thin bones of the characterization and not only give it solidity but sympathy and attraction. In a way, the film is more about Newman and Redford than it is about the people they play – or anything else. It celebrates their celebrity and stardom. It provides a rich context for their glamor to shine. It suggests a camaraderie between them which audiences, both male and female, obviously found highly seductive.

For a variety of reasons, "buddy movies" – films that lovingly explore the friendship between two men – were very

Left: *Big-time conman Gondorff is down on his luck when Hooker finds him staying in the brothel run by his girlfriend: but he makes a rapid recovery when he cheats the gangster in a poker game on the once-famous New York to Chicago train, the Twentieth Century.*

popular at this time. Fonda and Hopper in *Easy Rider* (1969), Voight and Hoffman in *Midnight Cowboy* (1969), Sutherland and Gould in *M*A*S*H* (1970), Hackman and Scheider in *The French Connection* (1971), McQueen and Hoffman in *Papillon* (1972) are only a few of the partnerships explored in films of this time. Whether the reason for this trend was commercial (two for the price of one), political (reassurance of male companionship and courage in a time of the unpopular Vietnam war), or sexual (the response of conservative, male-dominated Hollywood to the Women's Movement), Newman and Redford embodied it at its most handsome and least neurotic. Although one could take exception to its amorality and particularly at its celebration of conmanship at the time of Watergate, basically *The Sting* is simply designed to delight, and that it did.

Left: *Chicago, 1936; the elaborate plot (script by David S. Ward) revolves around a scheme devised by major-league conman Henry Gondorff (Paul Newman – left) and promising trainee Johnny Hooker (Robert Redford) to "fleece" the gangster who killed their friend. Gondorff sets up a phony gambling club and Hooker persuades the gangster that he can cheat Gondorff by getting race results early on the telegraph. When the big bet is made, the enraged Gondorff appears to shoot the treacherous Hooker and then be killed himself during an FBI raid. But all is not as it seems… and ends happily for the two triumphant buddies.*

Right: *Redford's performance was nominated for an Academy Award, though both he and Newman had had more acting opportunities in **Butch Cassidy and the Sundance Kid** (1969). Their on-screen rapport was based on a strong real-life friendship.*

Horror
THE EXORCIST (Hoya/WB 1973)
Director: William Friedkin

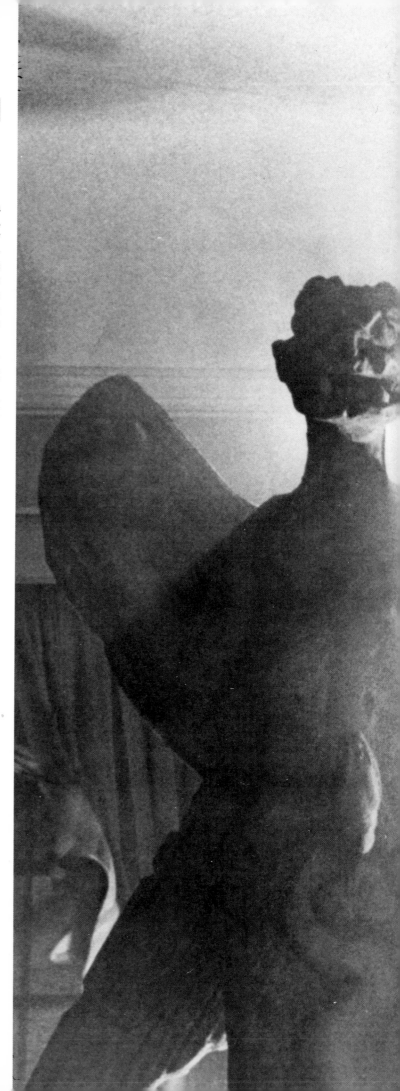

The Exorcist is one of those movies that became not simply a box-office smash hit but a site of cultural controversy. Analysis of it was undertaken not only by film critics but by anxious parents, child psychologists and eminent churchmen, whose combined views fanned a ferocious debate which contributed to the movie's earnings. It achieved such word-of-mouth reputation that not to have seen it was to be one step behind current fashion. As a female member of the audience told *Variety*: "I want to see what everybody is throwing up about."

The theme of *The Exorcist* is demonic possession, a subject that had proved to have great box-office potential in *Rosemary's Baby* (1968). In simple terms, it is a struggle of Good against Evil, an evil that has been implanted in a teenage girl, Regan (Linda Blair). But it goes way beyond that theme.

The immediate notoriety of the film was caused by the visual and verbal explicitness given to the girl's demonic state. The graphic horror – shaking rooms, swivelling heads, brightly-colored vomit, obscene language – undoubtedly helped the film's box-office impact. *The Exorcist* not only promises horrors: it delivers them, after an anxiously prolonged preparation (rather like the opening forty minutes of *Psycho*) in which nothing much happens. And although Good ultimately triumphs, Satan is the star of the film, as the villainous shark was to be the star of *Jaws*.

Profitable ambiguity
Many people read different meanings into the success of *The Exorcist*. Some feel it was pure escapism: by presenting Evil in such a banal and localized way, *The Exorcist* reassuringly deflected attention from other contemporary evils in society. It was an exorcism for the audience. Others feel it was a religious movie arguing that loss of faith can leave you susceptible to possession, and that, in essence, it is a vindication of the strength of the Roman Catholic Church – a kind of horror version of *Going My Way* (1944). Others see it as a reactionary movie in which the girl becomes possessed as a result of being the product of a broken family. In this reading, the villain of the film is the actress-mother (Ellen Burstyn), who feels guilty about her divorce and about her career – as James Baldwin put it, "in a word, her emancipation".

The Exorcist shows the power of the Devil in a society that is unquestionably weak and corrupt. Significantly, the evil is not simply approaching and must be resisted: it has already taken root and must be exorcized. Along with numerous, graphically explicit horror films of this period, *The Exorcist* is a crude and powerful expression of contemporary anxieties about the decline of family life, and the collapse of moral values. It cunningly hedges its bets: the outcome is hopeful, but, in the meantime, the Devil is given all the best tunes. Was *The Exorcist* exploitative commercialism at its most debased, or a fearful and responsible analysis of the power of evil and the capacity of a community to overcome it? The ambiguity did no harm at all to the film's popularity.

No-one rests easy once Regan is possessed by the Devil. **Above:** *she denounces her anxious family while,* **left***, her eventual savior Fr Damien Karras sets out to take on the Demon.*

Disaster Movie
THE TOWERING INFERNO (WB/Fox 1974)
Director: John Guillermin

The Towering Inferno is *Grand Hotel* in flames. A fire starts on the 81st floor of a huge tower building. Soon the flames are licking their way to floor 135 where top civic dignitaries are celebrating the building's construction. The movie had been financed jointly by Warner Brothers and 20th Century-Fox when it was discovered that they were individually adapting two very similar novels.

The screenwriter Stirling Silliphant, who had won an Oscar for the fine screenplay of *In the Heat of the Night* (1967), was brought in to combine the two and seems to have creamed off the highlights of each.

The movie came in the wake of hugely successful disaster movies like *The Poseidon Adventure* (1972) and *Earthquake* (1974), and exceeded their success. There were probably a number of reasons for this. *Inferno* has two big stars, Paul Newman and Steve McQueen, so the film can exploit what was left of the "buddy movie" formula: two blue-eyed boys fighting the flames together. The fire breaks out relatively early so that audiences are not left hanging on until the end for the thrills. Also it is the kind of thing we could all plausibly experience (more so than typhoon or earthquake): this gives it added immediacy and identification.

The Towering Inferno could be taken as an allegory of ambition and aspiration – the higher it gets, the hotter it gets, and the survivors will be the superstars (Paul Newman and Steve McQueen) rather than the more modestly talented (Jennifer Jones, Robert Wagner) who have clung onto their status by their fingernails. With a mixture of anxiety and relish, the plebeian audience watches this scorching allegory of success from the safe, less exciting vantage point of the ground floor. The story could also be interpreted as a modern version of the Titanic, in which man's technological arrogance (the tower building) is undercut by Nature (the fire), and man is finally saved by an elemental struggle between fire and water. Eyes, which at the beginning of the film gaze skywards in admiration of the building, finally gaze heavenwards in gratitude at God's mercy.

Worst fears overcome

Needless to say, Hollywood is too shrewd to give all the credit to Nature. The fire is actually caused by faulty wiring (Richard Chamberlain's wretched architect cutting corners and costs), and the people are saved through the expertise of fireman Steve McQueen and engineer Paul Newman. In fact, the film, like the other successful disaster movies, is a very deft blend of anxiety and reassurance. On the one hand, an audience's worst fears about the safety of tower buildings is shown: at the same time, the audience is flattered by the fact that its worst fears are confirmed. On the one hand, the disaster is a metaphor for a disaster-filled world, disasters which are created by humans but somehow seem beyond human control (nuclear fears are relevant here). On the other hand, it shows the capability of superstar humans to bring that disaster under control, and particularly shows the capability of our men in uniform for handling any disasters that our bureaucrats and politicians have contrived. We can safely leave them to sort things out and tell us what to do.

Left: *The world's tallest building goes up in flames and all because Richard Chamberlain,* **left inset,** *has installed cheap wiring.*

Above: *A helicopter rescue for those trapped in the scenic elevator, by order of the fire chief.*

The Towering Inferno is more of a warning than a disaster, the kind of thing that can happen without proper procedures and consultation and if economics take precedence over safety. But at the same time it demonstrates the ability of our fire-fighting forces, and promises (rather hopefully) responsible co-operation between the engineers and firemen in the future. Basically, audiences loved the spectacle of Paul Newman and Steve McQueen, spatially separated from the rest of the mainly passive victims, acting resourcefully and bravely on our behalf. "If you can't stand the heat, get out of the kitchen," said President Truman about the pressures and responsibilities of those in power. In a way, that is the message of *The Towering Inferno*. Newman and McQueen not only can stand the heat: they show it by *rescuing* the kitchen.

Suspense

JAWS (Zanuck-Brown/Universal 1975)
Director: Steven Spielberg

According to screenwriter William Goldman, the three most commercially *significant* Hollywood films are *Gone with the Wind*, *The Sound of Music*, and *Jaws*. The first represents the culmination of popular cinema at a certain high period of confidence by the industry in the audience. The significance of *The Sound of Music* was "because its phenomenal success paved the way for expensive imitations which almost destroyed Hollywood." *Jaws* was significant "because it changed everybody's thinking as to how large an audience there was out there."

There is nothing seemingly out of the ordinary in the subject matter of *Jaws*. A man-and-woman-eating shark is threatening the tourist trade of an American resort, and three men in a boat are sent out to destroy it. There is no doubt that the film is exceptionally well shot, Spielberg's direction being the most efficient manipulation of an audience since *Psycho*. He cunningly withholds a sight of the shark until quite late in the narrative; John Williams' music adds a grisly note of suspense, like an anxious heart-beat; and all the shocks (the first attack on the girl swimmer, the discovery of a victim in an underwater wreck, the first appearance of the shark behind the sheriff) are expertly timed. As Pauline Kael once remarked, a truly frightening movie has a fair chance of becoming a classic of a kind.

Biting at success
The movie was based on a novel by Peter Benchley, and the adaptation cut a sexual subplot so that it could concentrate exclusively on the action. It was heavily pre-sold, and, combined with the success of the book, it took off in a quite spectacular way. Ironically, in a movie that exposes the callousness of commercialism (the community of Amity wants to cover up news of the shark attacks for fear it might ruin their trade), *Jaws* was itself a triumph of uninhibited consumerist packaging. It frightened its summertime audience off the beaches and out of the swimming pools – and into the movie theaters. Within six weeks, one person in eight in America had seen it. When that kind of phenomenon occurs, it is no longer simply a successful movie: it is a deeply significant media event.

Various theories have been propounded to account for this success. In his book *Movies as Social Criticism*, J. C. Jarvis has suggested that "the movies are freer than a hidebound, home-centred, middle-class medium like television to explore the extremities of human experience, and they are hence more interesting to adolescents who are still, after all, exploring the possibilities and limits of experience." One can certainly apply this directly to *Jaws*. The audience that went to the movie was predominantly adolescent. Within a recognizable social context, the movie offered them the prospect of extraordinary adventure, something quite different from the expectations aroused by their home lives. For the novelist and historian, Gore Vidal, the success of a movie like *Jaws* lay simply in its escapism. "Such movies," said Vidal, "distract people from thoughts of the robbery and deceit to which they are subjected daily by oil companies, politicians and banks."

Explosive solution
Actually, *Jaws* might subconsciously have gained something of its power not simply from its escapism but from its contemporary relevance. Part of it is about political and commercial machinations. America was just emerging from Watergate. The first part of *Jaws* drops topically disquieting post-Watergate markers of political cover-up, notably in the Mayor's shady endeavor to conceal the danger of the shark. *Jaws* then veers into reassuringly rousing adventure. Intriguingly, the second half chooses to ignore the problem of the community's greed. It is almost as if the film is saying: "We have had enough self-analysis; let's not go into the *causes* of the problem, let's just eliminate the problem." So all the energy and hatred are displaced onto the hunt for the shark, which is not simply killed but annihilated.

Jaws is ultimately about the restoration of communal confidence after a massive trauma. America finally did not want answers for Watergate: it wanted to forget it, to blow it out of the water. The narrative strategy of *Jaws* seems closely akin to a national mood that wished to erase recent bad memories and to start afresh. The movie is an exorcism of tension and trauma, a purgation of paranoia. It is an ultimate affirmation of the capacity of the ordinary American male (implicitly, America) to find reserves of strength and resourcefulness he didn't know he possessed; and to get back to the business of living.

Jaws emptied the beaches as quickly as **Psycho** emptied motel showers. Here the Great White shark strikes for the first time. For a while it seems as if the monster has been caught, **left inset,** but shark expert Hooper (Richard Dreyfuss) knows better and tells police chief Roy Scheider, who eventually sets off, along with Robert Shaw, **right inset,** to annihilate evil.

Drama

ONE FLEW OVER THE CUCKOO'S NEST
(Fantasy/UA 1975)
Director: Milos Forman

Ken Kesey's *One Flew Over the Cuckoo's Nest* had been one of the cult novels of the sixties, a kind of horror-comic and authoritarian scream about an asylum inmate McMurphy who was always in conflict with the evil Nurse Ratched. Kirk Douglas had played McMurphy on stage and had acquired the movie rights, which had then passed to his son Michael. By the time filming was possible, Dad was too old for the role and times had changed. What to do with the material? Milos Forman was assigned to direct and immediately the material took on a different color. The specifically sixties "tripping" and "counterculture" elements in the original were eliminated. The characterization became stylized and more humanized, particularly in the case of Nurse Ratched, who becomes a more chilling but convincing conformist than the novel's misogynistic Mum devouring the souls of the "sons" in her charge, against the frantic opposition of "Father" McMurphy. The film turns into a more somber, sober comedy which also permits social criticism. Exiled from Czechoslovakia since 1968, Forman had no illusion about the lengths to which an institution (society) would go in order to ensure conformity in its members.

A ray of hope

For a while it is McMurphy's energy that dominates the picture. When the television is switched off, he improvises a manic commentary on the World Series for the inmates that seems more vivid and exciting than the real thing. (More dangerous too: he is liberating their imagination.) In a basketball game between the male nurses and the inmates, he strategically uses the huge Indian (Will Sampson) to win the game. The audience is tremendously lifted and amused by such instances, which make the eventual fate of McMurphy – lobotomy for his attempted murder of the nurse – all the more horrifying. But the film ends on a triumphant note. In a sense picking up the torch that McMurphy has let fall, the Indian takes the marble stand that McMurphy has earlier tried to lift, hurls it through the window, and runs for freedom. "Never leave an audience feeling empty" is a trusted Hollywood maxim: the optimistic finale of *Cuckoo's Nest* might well have made all the difference between the movie's success or failure.

They all tried

American films are never more characteristic and committed than in those moments when they are celebrating the individual or nonconformist. They have always had their key actors to do it. It was Cagney in the thirties, Brando and James Dean in the fifties, and, in the seventies, it was pre-eminently Jack Nicholson. He has all the volatility, anarchy and humor of the born rebel. All of his great performances in the decade – *Five Easy Pieces* (1970), *The Last Detail* (1973), *Chinatown* (1974), *Cuckoo's Nest* – derive in part from his characterization in *Easy Rider*. They were all movies about doomed rebels who try to break down a corrupt system, fail, and are brought brutally back into line. But, as McMurphy says in *Cuckoo's Nest*: "At least I tried."

Right: *He attempts to liven up group therapy sessions by trying to rouse the unresponsive patients to protest against the system.*

Below: *Randle P. McMurphy (Jack Nicholson), transferred from a penal work farm to a mental hospital, challenges the exasperatingly dictatorial regime of Nurse Ratched (Louise Fletcher).*

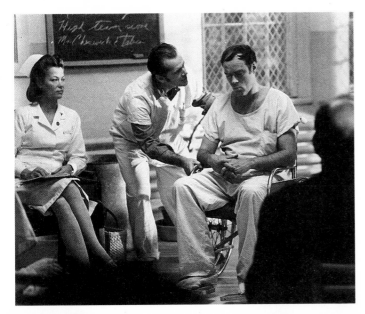

Cuckoo's Nest became the first film since *It Happened One Night* (1934) to make a clean sweep of all the major Oscars – Best Film, Best Actor (Nicholson), Best Actress (Louise Fletcher), Best Director, Best Screenplay. A word should be said for Louise Fletcher's blood-chilling performance as Nurse Ratched, less overtly monstrous than in the novel, but more formidable and fearful. "She is dangerous," said Forman, "because she really believes what she is doing. I have seen this situation, and I know that authority in trouble will sacrifice anything and anyone to prove its point." We can all put names and faces to the Nurse Ratcheds in our society.

The film polarizes the conflict rather differently from the novel. It is not Dad versus Mum, or Sane versus Insane (to show the relativity of so-called madness), but commitment to self-definition over rigid commitment to institution or ideology. Freed from the limitations of its sixties ambience, the movie became a timeless American celebration of the rebel hero. It scored because it was made by a director who understood the theme and performed to the hilt by the one actor of the time who could play it better than anyone.

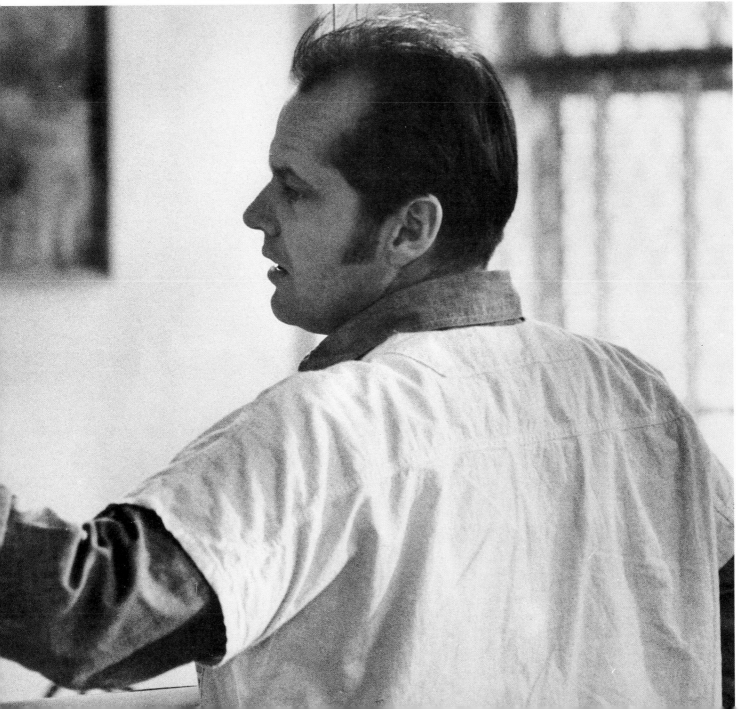

STAR WARS (Lucasfilm/Fox 1977)
Director: George Lucas

CLOSE ENCOUNTERS OF THE THIRD KIND (Columbia/EMI 1977)
Director: Steven Spielberg

Star Wars initially had difficulty in getting off the ground. It had been turned down by Universal and United Artists, and it was three years between inception and the beginning of shooting, by which time the movie had been picked up by 20th Century-Fox. According to producer Gary Kurtz, there was trouble over the title. The studio argued that no film with "star" or "war" in the title had ever made a lot of money and the combination might be disastrous. Director George Lucas insisted that there were eight million dollars worth of science-fiction freaks that would go to anything called *Star Wars*, and the additional audience should cover the movie's budget of around eleven million dollars and ensure a tidy profit. By the end of 1980 the movie had grossed $510 million on world-wide release. This is excluding the massive profits from artefacts inspired by the movie, including books, bubble-gum, T-shirts, watches and breakfast cereal.

A modern fairytale
Star Wars combines the elements which had characterized the two most popular science-fiction films of the previous decade. It has the sophisticated technology of *2001* (1968) and the straightforward fantasy adventure of *Planet of the Apes* (1968). Gary Kurtz described it as "an homage to all the action adventure fantasies of the movies – in particular, the science-fiction serials of the thirties like Flash Gordon." For all the deep political significance that has been read into the movie's battle between the mystical Force and the black-clad Jedi, it is basically designed as a fairytale for modern youth. Its massive appeal is partly to do with its creation of an individual fantasy world of heroes and beasts, and partly to do with its incorporation of the most modern technology into the most old-fashioned of morality plays. The special effects are not simply part of *Star Wars*: they are its *raison d'être*.

Toy maker
Many of the critics were distinctly unimpressed. *Newsweek* claimed that "it lacks story (as opposed to action), characters (as opposed to cartoon figures) and any real emotional resonance." That is not only true but it is also an explanation of its success. After a traumatic period in America's recent history, the movie offered total escapism that is emptied of all significance. Emotions are limited to the callowness of Luke Skywalker (Mark Hamill), the cynicism of Han Solo (Harrison Ford), the coyness of Princess Leia (Carrie Fisher) and the creaky interplay of R2-D2 and C-3PO, who are a kind of robotic Laurel and Hardy. Apparently Lucas himself does not think too highly of the film, but this unpretentiousness is quite appealing. "I'm very much akin to a toy maker," he said once. "If I wasn't a film-maker, I'd probably to be a toy maker. I like to make things move and I like to make them myself." *Star Wars* is a gigantic toy, a film about "cosmic pinball" (as one critic described it), a proposition that life and the future are all a kind of vast game in space. The enormous success of

Main picture: *The apprehensive Luke Skywalker keeping an eye out for enemy aliens.*

its frivolous attitude to cosmic warfare has its alarming implications, but it might be better to take it as the new myth of the modern age, in which the heroes and villains of the old-fashioned westerns are now dressed in space suits.

Hard on the heels of *Star Wars* came Steven Spielberg's *Close Encounters of the Third Kind* (1977), a film about the landing of UFOs on earth. In contrast to the Cold War science-fiction movies of the fifties and the intellectual pessimism of *2001, Close Encounters* is a hymn to the grandeur rather than the terror of the unknown. Advanced technology assists towards a communication with extra-terrestrials that inspires a religious sense of awe. Language is less important for communication than music and visual signs, a lesson Spielberg applies with great skill to his movie.

Like most Spielberg heroes, Richard Dreyfuss in *Close Encounters* is swept up in an extraordinary adventure that offers a release from his boring humdrum existence. For many, the escape into pure fantasy is the essence of the cinema's appeal, which is the reason that audiences identify so intensely with the hero's predicament. The awesome landing of the alien spacecraft occupies the last forty minutes of the film, and is the ultimate special effect of seventies cinema. This is the triumph of technology with a vengeance, but also with a heart. Man makes contact with aliens from another planet, and audiences renew contact with the concept of cinema as the magic palace.

"We have made contact!" Tucked away in the mountains of Wyoming, scientists in **Close Encounters of the Third Kind** *watch a gigantic alien spaceship, ablaze with flashing lights, slowly descend to earth for their first meeting with apparently friendly creatures from outer space.*

Musical
SATURDAY NIGHT FEVER (Paramount 1977)
Director: John Badham

GREASE (Paramount 1978)
Director: Randal Kleiser

In the late seventies, Hollywood made a belated discovery – namely, that the audience that mainly bought records were of the same eighteen to twenty-five age group that went to the movies. Why not exploit this connection to the mutual benefit of both?

The person who did this with stunning success was musical impresario-turned-film producer, Robert Stigwood, who transformed an article by Nik Cohn about the culture and sociology of the contemporary disco dancing phenomenon into *Saturday Night Fever*. The hero is Tony Manero (John Travolta) whose routine life during the day is transcended by his stunning skill on the dance floor at night. The theme is not dissimilar to *Rocky* (1976) – the hero breaking free of his working-class existence – which might account for the favorable response to the movie. In fact, the picture was originally prepared by the director of *Rocky*, John G. Avildsen, but disagreements over the script led to Avildsen's replacement by a young director, John Badham, who gives enormous color and bounce to the material. The other major feature of the film is the stylish, high-stepping Oscar-nominated performance of Travolta that had younger audiences in transports of delight.

The three M's
On top of that, the film was extremely skilfully marketed. The launch was described as follows by the rock magazine, *Rolling Stone*: "In late September, the Stigwood organization released a Bee Gees single, 'How Deep Is Your Love", which reached number one. In early November, the album was released a month before the film, but timed to take advantage of the hit single, the holiday season and a three-minute

Right: *Grease* is the word – Sandy (Olivia Newton-John) recalls her summer romance **(far right)** with Danny Zucco (John Travolta).

trailer being shown in 1500 theaters hyping both the film and the album." The record had sold nearly a million before the release of the film: immediately after its release in December, it sold three-quarters of a million in four days. Asked why the soundtrack was such a success, Maurice Gibb of the Bee Gees responded, plausibly enough: "It was a combination of the two, John and us. The music made the film and the film made the music. The music, the movie and, of course, the marketing."

Grease inevitably capitalized on Travolta's sudden and stunning popularity. The stage show had been a big hit on Broadway since 1972, anyway, though Ned Tannen of Universal commented: "It had been around for five years and nobody could give it away." Travolta made the difference and so did the times. The appeal of the show lay in its nostalgic look back to the fifties – the early years of rock 'n' roll and an age of relative innocence before Vietnam and Watergate. The movie takes a seventies look at the fantasies of the fifties, affectionate but ironic. Older members of the audience could respond to the profusion of supporting character actors, including Sid Caesar, Eve Arden, Joan Blondell and Stockard Channing. However, the film is characterized especially by the absence of parent figures, and by the sheer presence of its young stars, the vigorous John Travolta and the angelic Olivia Newton-John, the former playing Elvis Presley to the latter's Sandra Dee. It proved a charismatic combination.

Left: *Tony (John Travolta) wins first prize on the disco floor with Stephanie (Karen Gorney) in* **Saturday Night Fever***.*
Below: *Lost in the subway after the death of his friend.*

Adventure
SUPERMAN: THE MOVIE (Salkind/WB 1978)
Director: Richard Donner

According to the creators of Superman, Jerry Siegel and Joe Shuster, the inspiration for the super-hero basically stemmed from the silent films. The Douglas Fairbanks of *Robin Hood* (1922) and *The Black Pirate* (1926) gave them the idea for the dash and pose of Superman, while the screen persona of Harold Lloyd was their reference point for the bumbling, bespectacled Clark Kent (Superman's earthly disguise). Although many have speculated on the popularity of the comic strip (the acerbic cultural critic Leslie Fiedler has suggested that readers responded most to Superman's supreme act of heroism in staying out of the clutches of women), Siegel and Shuster thought that the character's basic appeal was that he could achieve the impossible. When they sold the first Superman story in the thirties they were paid sixty dollars. When the film came to be made in the late seventies, its budget (at a conservative estimate) was around fifty million dollars.

To say that the film was heavily pre-sold would be one of the decade's understatements. The merchandising of Superman products was quite awesome – from books to lunch boxes, from posters to cereal bowls, from badges to pajamas. But, as modern Hollywood has sometimes found to its cost (the 1981 film of *Annie* is an example), such merchandizing can disastrously backfire if the film does not live up to expectations. Fortunately, Superman delighted audiences everywhere.

The structure of the movie is relatively straightforward, setting up who the hero is, how he comes to earth, and what happens when he pits his super powers against earthquakes, tidal waves and uninhibited villainy. In fact, the three parts, although separately well done, tend not to hang together. The awesome Krypton sequences contrast with the innocent Americana of the boy's early life, which in turn contrasts with the exuberant comedy of Superman's enterprises. But an imposing performance by Marlon Brando as Jor-El gets things off to a flying start, Gene Hackman's Lex Luthor is a sprightly villain, and Margot Kidder's Lois Lane a spunky and attractive heroine. But what especially enhanced the film were the special effects and the casting of Christopher Reeve as Superman.

The cinema of wonder

"You'll believe a man can fly," said the publicity. Closely supervised by director Richard Donner and his team of expert technicians, the effects ensure that this is so. There is magic in the air when Superman goes into his solo flights, whether apprehending a cat burglar, or rescuing Lois from a fall from a tower block. The material could have collapsed into unfortunate parody in the wrong hands. But the writing team was exceptionally strong, including Tom Mankiewicz, Mario Puzo (author of *The Godfather*) and David Newman and Robert Benton (authors of *Bonnie and Clyde*). Donner, who had just had a huge hit with the horror film *The Omen* (1976), took great care to avoid parody on the one hand and ponderousness on the other. It is not an American satire (Richard Lester was to take it further in that direction when he made *Superman II* and *Superman III*), but a contribution

to the cinema of wonder. Technically, Donner had achieved that. But could the actor do what the director wanted – "play it as straight as you can within the fable"?

Apparently, when Marlon Brando rang James Caan to enquire incredulously why Caan had turned down an offer of four million dollars to play the role of Superman, Caan had replied: "It's okay for you, you don't have to wear that costume." Christopher Reeve wears the costume, and the role, exceptionally well. As Donner wanted, he takes the role straight. Reeve saw Superman as a warm and humorous person, "a solitary man with incredible powers, trying to fit into his adopted planet." But the real fun, Reeve thought, was in playing the bumbling Clark Kent, which he does with genuine comic assurance.

When producer Ilya Salkind was asked to explain the success of *Superman: The Movie*, he said: "It's largely because of the spirit of the legend. Everybody wants to fly, everybody wants to feel free, and totally on top of the world. In that sense, there's something of Superman in all of us." Christopher Reeve had an interesting, alternative explanation. He thought audiences identified more with Clark Kent, and that this more human dimension to the character gave him the necessary extra sympathy. The aim of having an audience leave the theater on wings was amply fulfilled.

Bottom: *Marlon Brando as Jor-El and wife Lara perish on the exploding planet Krypton, having sent son Superman to Earth. Here he astounds his foster parents* (**inset**) *by picking up real-life cars instead of toy ones. Later he discovers the excitement of an earthly kiss with ace reporter Lois Lane* (**far left**).

1. Gone with the Wind (1939)
2. Star Wars (1977)
3. The Sound of Music (1965)
4. The Ten Commandments (1956)
5. Jaws (1975)
6. Ben-Hur (1959)
7. The Godfather (1972)
8. Around the World in 80 Days (1956)
9. Doctor Zhivago (1965)
10. Grease (1978)
11. The Robe (1953)
12. The Sting (1973)
13. The Exorcist (1973)
14. The Graduate (1967)
15. Close Encounters of the Third Kind (1977)
16. Superman (1978)

Left inset: *The Sound of Music.*
Top : *The Sting.*
Below : *Doctor Zhivago.*
Opposite page: *Star Wars.*

ALL-TIME BOX-OFFICE HITS

The most reliable list of All-Time Box-Office Hits up to 1980 is provided in the British book *Anatomy of the Movies.* Unlike the lists in *Variety,* for example, it does not simply list the movies according to box-office receipts, but takes into account the effects of inflation and varying ticket prices etc. However, it acknowledges that it cannot reflect profitability: the takings of *Cleopatra* (1963) conceal its much higher production costs, and the takings of *Jaws II* (1978) do not reflect the enormous amount spent on advertising campaigns. Nevertheless, with these provisos, the following are the *Top 50 Box-Office Films* up to the end of the seventies.

17. Saturday Night Fever (1977)
18. Snow White and the Seven Dwarfs (1937)
19. West Side Story (1961)
20. Cleopatra (1963)
21. Mary Poppins (1964)
22. This Is the Army (1943)
23. Love Story (1970)
24. South Pacific (1958)
25. The Best Years of Our Lives (1946)
26. One Flew Over the Cuckoo's Nest (1976)
27. The Greatest Show on Earth (1952)
28. Duel in the Sun (1947)
    The Towering Inferno (1974)
30. National Lampoon's Animal House (1978)
31. The Bridge on the River Kwai (1957)
    Goldfinger (1964)
    Thunderball (1965)

Main picture: *The Best Years of Our Lives.*

Center: *One Flew over the Cuckoo's Nest.*

Above left: *Smokey and the Bandit.*
Above: *Sergeant York.*
Left and right: *Around the World in 80 Days.*
Above right: *The Graduate.*

34. From Here to Eternity (1953)
    Smokey and the Bandit (1977)
36. Airport (1970)
37. Rocky (1976)
38. The Longest Day (1962)
39. Sergeant York (1941)
    White Christmas (1954)
41. The Poseidon Adventure (1972)
42. Going My Way (1944)
43. Butch Cassidy and the Sundance Kid (1969)
44. Quo Vadis (1952)
45. American Graffiti (1973)
46. It's a Mad, Mad, Mad, Mad World (1963)
47. For Whom the Bell Tolls (1943)
48. The Bells of St Mary's (1945)
    Spartacus (1960)
50. Jaws II (1978)

CHAPTER SIX:

CONCLUSION

MODERN BOX-OFFICE TRENDS: THE EIGHTIES

The good news for the industry is that the force is still with George Lucas and Steven Spielberg. Lucas' *Star Wars* sagas have continued with unabated success. *The Empire Strikes Back* (1980), directed by Irvin Kershner, and *Return of the Jedi* (1983), directed by Richard Marquand, were the most commercially successful movies of their year. Everything Spielberg has touched recently has turned to gold. With Lucas, he has created a new (or very old) hero in Indiana Jones who, in *Raiders of the Lost Ark* (1981) and *Indiana Jones and the Temple of Doom* (1984), has gone through wild, athletic and adventuresome escapades that resemble the old movie serials of the thirties in everything but budget. Spielberg's mantle as the Disney of the new age has been particularly confirmed by *E.T.* (1982), in which an extra-terrestrial stranded on earth brings a Peter Pan-like fantasy into the world of middle America children.

In an attractive gesture, Spielberg's productions of *Poltergeist* (1982) and, particularly, *Gremlins* (1984) permitted directors Tobe Hooper and Joe Dante to satirize his wholesome middle America world by allowing mischievous demons to run amok in it. After the apocalyptic visions of the seventies, both films have brought geniality and humor back into the horror film, as has John Landis' *An American Werewolf in London* (1981). David Lynch's *The Elephant Man* (1980) even brought humanity back into the formula as well. The combination of horror and *National Lampoon* humor, allied to special effects of which Lucas would have been

Top inset: *Indiana (Harrison Ford) fights off an assassin in* **Indiana Jones and the Temple of Doom** *(1984).*

Left inset: *Gertie (Drew Barrymore) makes friends with the lovable* **E.T. The Extra-Terrestrial** *(1982).*

Main picture: *Elliott and E.T. fly through the night.*

proud, made *Ghostbusters* (1984) the unexpected box-office sensation of the year.

The eighties have tended to consolidate gains made in the seventies rather than to initiate any new trends equivalent to the rash of disaster movies, buddy movies, or rogue cop movies that characterized the early years of the previous decade. Instead, there has been a steady series of straightforward sequels. *Jaws, Amityville Horror* and *Friday the 13th* have all gone successfully into 3-D. Sylvester Stallone's Rocky has continued his successful defense of the American Dream. In further adventures, Superman has seen off the threat of superpowers from his old planet and a malevolent giant computer from our own. James Bond shows no signs of retiring. We have had three *Halloweens,* two *Smokey and the Bandits,* two *Cannonball Runs,* two *Conans,* and two blobs of *Grease. Airplane!* (1980) satirized disaster movies so joyously that it made almost as much money as the films it lampooned, and quickly gave birth to a sequel.

Nowadays, many movies seem to build the possibility of a sequel into the structure of the original, just in case it turns out to be an unexpected smash hit. When in doubt, go back to a proven formula. Clint Eastwood reprised Dirty Harry when the public stayed away from his *Honky Tonk Man* (1983). *Psycho II* (1983) revisits Norman Bates after he has been let out of the asylum. *2001* is given a very different atmospheric treatment in *2010* (1984): the cool scepticism of the former compared with the desperate Utopianism of the latter says a great deal about the difference in spirit between the sixties and the eighties – their movies and their worlds.

Left: *Superman (Christopher Reeve) to the rescue of God, America and mom's apple pie in Richard Lester's tongue-in-cheek* **Superman II** *(1980).*

Top inset: *Harold Ramis, Dan Aykroyd and Bill Murray, the trio of scientists who hit the headlines as the fearless* **Ghostbusters** *(1984).*

Above: *Coming in on a wing and a prayer, stewardess Elaine (Julie Hagerty) and automatic pilot struggle to keep the* **Airplane!** *(1980) on course.*

Reflecting the times

Movies have always been very sensitive barometers of national mood. It is not surprising that American movies now, unlike those of the early seventies, tend to be conservative and traditional rather than radical and innovative. The American Dream has come back into the national cinema with a fervor that has not been seen since the thirties. Successes like John Landis' *Trading Places* (1983) and Barry Levinson's *The Natural* (1984) have something of the spirit and emotion of Frank Capra. Sentiment is encouraged. Weepies like *Ordinary People* (1980) and *Terms of Endearment* (1983), two Oscar-winning directing debuts from Robert Redford and James L. Brooks, have been exceedingly popular exploitations of family feeling. For the first time ever,

the theme of old age made money (*On Golden Pond* – 1982).

In the Reagan era, Hollywood has more than come to terms with traumatic events like the Vietnam war: a popular movie like *Uncommon Valor* (1984) can all but imply that the war was a heroic victory. Military themes are in again, whether comic *(Stripes)*, romantic *(An Officer and a Gentleman)* or serious *(Taps)*, and this affirmation of national pride is rewarded with tremendous popular acclaim. Thoughtful movies that have been critical of various aspects of American domestic or political policies, such as *Rollover* (1982), *Missing* (1982), *Under Fire* (1983) and *Daniel* (1983), have not found favor with the American public, who seem sick of the kind of anguish and self-examination that tore America apart between 1968 and 1973.

Left: *Dan Aykroyd, disguised as Santa Claus, and Eddie Murphy in John Landis' successful comedy* **Trading Places** *(1983).*

Terms of Endearment *(1983), starring Shirley MacLaine and Jack Nicholson* **(right)**, *took the American passion for soap opera out of the television and on to the big screen. The marriage of Emma (Debra Winger,* **above***) and Flap, terminated by her death from cancer, brought out as many handkerchiefs as did* **Love Story**.

Out of tune

Accordingly, some of the more eccentric and anarchic directing talents of the seventies have had difficulty in tuning in to the current decade. The guru of movie brats, Francis Ford Coppola, has struggled to make an impact, either with avant-garde works like *Rumble Fish* (1983) or huge, hollow genre studies like *One from the Heart* (1982) and *The Cotton Club* (1984). Satirists like Ritchie and Mazursky and original oddballs like Scorsese, Altman and De Palma have also found it hard going. Whatever the reasons, it is sad when movies as stylish, subtle and satirical as Phil Kaufman's *The Right Stuff* (1983), Jack Clayton's *Something Wicked This Way Comes* (1983) and Martin Scorsese's *The King of Comedy* (1983) fail so abjectly to find the audience they were anticipating.

Two genres that have yet to rediscover an impetus in the eighties are the western and the musical. Michael Cimino's *Heaven's Gate* (1981) almost killed off a genre as well as United Artists, and few of the stars of the eighties seem to have the persona to take over the cowboy mantle of a John Wayne. Yet several new westerns are appearing in 1985, including one by Clint Eastwood and one by talented newcomer Lawrence Kasdan, who has made an impact with his first two films, *Body Heat* (1981) and *The Big Chill* (1983), so maybe the genre is reviving. After the failure of the much-trumpeted *Annie* (1981), the traditional musical has been displaced by dance musicals that have aimed to exploit youthful fashions. *Flashdance* (1983) has been the most popular. John Travolta recovered some of his luster after his starring role in Stallone's *Staying Alive* (1983). Strangely, Travolta's following seems to desert him whenever he leaves the dance floor.

Above: *In Sidney Poitier's successful comedy* **Stir Crazy** *(1980), Skip (Gene Wilder) is sentenced to 125 years for a bank robbery he did not commit, along with his partner Harry, played by Richard Pryor. But Skip turns out to have natural-born genius as a cowboy on the mechanical bucking bull, which gives rise to an ingenious escape plan at the rodeo…*

Below and right: *The erotic Jennifer Beals and lookalike in* **Flashdance** *(1983).*

Above: *An encounter with a paranormal phenomenon (not the lady librarian) in the New York Public Library gives three parapsychologists of dubious scientific standing (Bill Murray, Harold Ramis, Dan Aykroyd) the idea of becoming **Ghostbusters** when their university funding is summarily cut off.*

Left: *Murray in full cry, hot in pursuit of the infernal spirits – and bedevilled Sigourney Weaver.*

After the return of the symphonic film score in the seventies, the new decade has slipped back into the old sixties habit: the use of promotional pop music, however incongruous, over the soundtrack of a movie to draw in an audience. The success of *Ghostbusters*, *Woman in Red* (1984) and *Against All Odds* (1984) might well have something to do with their pop soundtracks and the video promotion that publicized them: it is equally evident that these pop soundtracks had very little to do with the rhythms and themes of the movies.

This is one dubious area of the movie industry's concerted appeal to the teenage market that now constitutes the major part of the movie audience. Another is the generally low level of current American comedy, where crude slapstick seems to have taken the place of verbal wit. *Porky's* (1982) and *Police Academy* (1983) have not much more than energy to recommend them but have taken eight times the money of Woody Allen gems like *Zelig* (1983) and *Broadway Danny Rose* (1984). Nevertheless, one of the finds of the decade so far has been Eddie Murphy, justifying his star status in *Beverly Hills Cop* (1984) by carrying a slight comedy vehicle to enormous box-office success. Also, the runaway success of a comedy like *Tootsie* (1982) is encouraging. Certainly it had calculatedly commercial ingredients like the gimmick of Dustin Hoffman in drag and a hit song. But is also had attention to character and the ability to develop a humorous concept with due regard for logical structure and inventive incident.

*Michael (Dustin Hoffman) does not want to become a woman in **Tootsie** (1982). He just wants work as an actor and no one will hire him as a man because he's impossible to work with. But as Dorothy...*

Plus and minus

The negative side of the current box-office scene is the determination to find the one blockbuster that will break the $150-$200 million barrier. It means that everything is staked on that and as a result a lot of good, smaller films which might need more careful nurturing have gone to the wall. (This is one of the negative legacies of the *Jaws/Star Wars* syndrome.)

The positive side is that the potential audience for movies seems larger than ever, in spite of and even because of the alternative claims of television, video and cable. There is still room for maneuver in the industry for experienced moviemakers such as Lumet, Penn, Kubrick, Frankenheimer and the evergreen John Huston, as well as opportunities for precocious talents with low-budget cult thrillers like Joel Coen's *Blood Simple* (1984). Exceptional actors and actres-

ses like Robert De Niro, Al Pacino, Meryl Streep and Jessica Lange encouragingly command attention at the box-office. Who could have predicted that a movie without stars and about Mozart, Milos Forman's *Amadeus* (1984), would sweep the board at the Oscars and also show a healthy profit? Or that the 77-year-old David Lean, making his first film for fifteen years, would have a potential winner with *A Passage to India* (1984)?

The instinct of a talented, experienced, obsessional filmmaker might still be more reliable than computer predictions or market forces. "There is no formula for success," said the director Nicholas Ray, "but there is a formula for failure, and that is trying to please everybody." Long may the movies encourage diversity, and be supported in that endeavor by their audiences.

Top left: *While Mozart (Tom Hulce) plays like an angel, it was F. Murray Abraham as Salieri (not in picture) who won the Oscar for* **Amadeus** *(1984).*

Above: *Adela Quested (Judy Davis) and her prospective mother-in-law Mrs Moore (Peggy Ashcroft) have taken* **A Passage to India** *in David Lean's prestigious 1984 production. The journey offers more than any could have expected, including death, a rape charge, and reconciled differences between the Europeans and Indians – unlike E.M. Forster's novel which stresses the irreconcilable conflict between East and West.*
Right: *Victor Bannerjee as Dr Aziz.*

PICTURE CREDITS

The Cinema Bookshop 34, 35 **Joel Finler** Front cover, inset top, inset center bottom, back cover inset center, half title, 7, 8 top, 10, 11, 11 inset, 13, 15, 16 bottom, 18, 19 bottom, 21 bottom, 24, 27 inset, 37 inset, 39 inset, 41 bottom, 42 top, 43, 45, 46-47, 48 top, 48 left, 49 bottom, 50-51, 54-55, 59, 68-69, 70-71, 72-73, 73, 74, 75, 76, 77, 78-79, 80, 81, 82, 83 inset, 86, 87, 90, 91 inset, 92, 93 bottom, 94, 95 top, 97, 98-99, 100 inset, 104-105, 106-107, 112, 116-117, 117, 118 bottom right, 123 bottom, 125 inset, 128-129 bottom, 129, 130, 131, 134, 136, 138-139, 142-143, 142, 144 center, 145 bottom, 153 top right, 153 top left, 154 center, 155, 156-157, 157, 158, 159, 161, 162-163, 166-167, 178 bottom, 179, 182-183, 182-183 inset, 184, 185, 186 bottom, 187, 188, 189 **Flashbacks** 14 bottom **Ronald Grant Archive** 9, 12 top, 14 top, 88, 103 bottom, 120-121, 150-151 **Kobal Collection** front cover main picture and inset center top, back cover main picture, contents page, 6, 12 bottom, 17, 19 top, 20, 21 top, 22, 23, 24 inset, 25, 26-27, 27, 28, 29, 30-31, 31, 32-33, 32, 36-37, 36 inset, 38, 39, 40, 41 top, 42 bottom, 44, 46, 48 bottom, 49 top, 51, 52, 53, 56, 57, 58, 60, 61, 62-63, 63, 64-65, 66, 67, 69, 72, 83, 84, 84-85, 88-89, 91, 93 top, 95 bottom, 96-97, 98, 102, 103 top, 107 inset, 108-109, 110-111, 111 inset, 113, 114, 114-115, 115 inset, 116, 118 bottom left, 119, 120 inset, 122, 123 top, 124-125, 126-127, 128-129 top, 132-133, 133 inset, 135, 136-137, 137, 140, 141, 143, 144 top, 144 bottom, 145 top, 146 bottom, 147, 149 top left, 151, 153 bottom, 158, 160-161, 164-165, 164, 166 bottom, 168-169, 168, 171, 174-175, 174 left inset, 175, 176-177 inset, 178 top left, 178 top right, 188-189, endpapers **National Film Archive** 176-177 **Rex Features** front cover bottom inset, bottom inset, back cover top inset, title page, 8 bottom, 118 top right, 124 top **Frank Spooner** 121 inset.

Many of the illustrations come from stills issued to publicize films made or distributed by the following companies:–
A.A./Bronston, **Columbia**/ Brabourne-Goodwyn/Delphi/ Frankovitch/ G.W./ Horizon/ Kramer/ Orion/ Pollack/ Preminger/ Raybert/ Raster/ Reitman/ Spiegel/ Weinstein, **David O. Selznick, Walt Disney, First National**/ Chaplin, **G.F.D.**/ The Archers/ Rank, Magna/ S.P. Enterprises, **MGM**/ Aron/ Hyman/ Kubrick/ Ponti, **Omni-Zeotrope, Orion**/ Zantz, **Paramount**/ Afran/ Brooks/ DeMille/ Embassy/ Folsey-Russo/ Hitchcock/ Koch/ Landis/ Lucasfilm/ Minski-Millar/ Polygram/ Shamley/ Stigwood, **PEA, RKO**/ Liberty films, **Twentieth Century Fox**/ Argyle/ Aspen/ Brandywine/ Campanile/ Kent/ Lucasfilm/ Warner, **United Artist**/ Constantin/ Embassy/ Eon/ Fantasy/ Hecht-Hill-Lancaster/ Jolly/ Kramer/ Millar/ Mirisch/ Ocean/ Selznick/ Todd/ Woodfall, **Universal International**/ Bryna/ EMI/ Spielberg/ Zanuck-Brown, **Warner-Seven Arts**/ Feldman, **Warner Brothers**/ Hoya/ Luft/ Salking.

Multimedia Publications (UK) Limited has endeavored to observe the legal requirements with regard to the rights of suppliers of photographic material.